Families and Parenting

Series Editor: Cara Acred

Volume 257

Independence Educational Publishers

First published by Independence Educational Publishers

The Studio, High Green

Great Shelford

Cambridge CB22 5EG

England

© Independence 2014

British Library Cataloguing in Publication Data

Independence

British Library Cataloguing in Publication Data

Families and parenting. -- (Issues ; 257)

1. Parenting. 2. Families.

I. Series II. Acred, Cara editor of compilation.

306.8'74-dc23

ISBN-13: 9781861686688

Printed in Great Britain

MWL Print Group Ltd

Contents

Introduction

Families and Parenting is Volume 257 in the ISSUES series. The aim of the series is to offer current, diverse information about important issues in our world, from a UK perspective.

ABOUT FAMILIES AND PARENTING

According to a report by Scottish Widows, 'Our families shape our lives in every sense'. But what does today's family structure look like? This books explores the different definitions of 'family' that exist in modern-day Britain and considers the issues faced by today's parents. It also looks at the complicated topic of family finances and the trials and tribulations encountered by teenage parents.

OUR SOURCES

Titles in the **ISSUES** series are designed to function as educational resource books, providing a balanced overview of a specific subject.

The information in our books is comprised of facts, articles and opinions from many different sources, including:

⇨ Newspaper reports and opinion pieces

⇨ Website factsheets

⇨ Magazine and journal articles

⇨ Statistics and surveys

⇨ Government reports

⇨ Literature from special interest groups.

A NOTE ON CRITICAL EVALUATION

Because the information reprinted here is from a number of different sources, readers should bear in mind the origin of the text and whether the source is likely to have a particular bias when presenting information (or when conducting their research). It is hoped that, as you read about the many aspects of the issues explored in this book, you will critically evaluate the information presented.

It is important that you decide whether you are being presented with facts or opinions. Does the writer give a biased or unbiased report? If an opinion is being expressed, do you agree with the writer? Is there potential bias to the 'facts' or statistics behind an article?

ASSIGNMENTS

In the back of this book, you will find a selection of assignments designed to help you engage with the articles you have been reading and to explore your own opinions. Some tasks will take longer than others and there is a mixture of design, writing and research-based activities that you can complete alone or in a group.

FURTHER RESEARCH

At the end of each article we have listed its source and a website that you can visit if you would like to conduct your own research. Please remember to critically evaluate any sources that you consult and consider whether the information you are viewing is accurate and unbiased.

Useful weblinks

www.4children.org.uk

www.barnardos.org.uk

www.centreformodernfamily.com

www.centreforsocialjustice.org.uk

www.familyandchildcaretrust.org

www.familylives.org.uk

www.gingerbread.org.uk

www.nspcc.org.uk

www.oneplusone.org.uk

www.oxfam.org.uk

www.stonewall.org.uk

www.worldfamilymap.org

The modern British family

Loving but frustrating, supportive yet argumentative – our families make us who we are.

An extract from the report by Scottish Widows

Our families shape our lives in every sense, from the argument we had this morning to the hope of a visit of a loved one. Yet, we don't often consider the size, structure, shape and attitudes we have towards our own family or what we would view as a 'normal' family in today's Britain. In this report, we hope to shed new light on the subject by not only exploring the architecture of family, but also our attitudes towards it. Can we live alone and still be part of a family? Do unmarried couples with children or gay couples constitute a 'proper' family? Are our changes in attitude a positive force for good, or are we just accepting a poorer future for all?

This report, produced by Scottish Widows Centre for the Modern Family, will be the first of many to provide insights into attitudes towards family in Britain today. Rather than offering answers at this stage, this report, and the research it reflects, asks important questions. It is the springboard for further, more detailed research, discussion and investigation by the Centre for the Modern Family, which hopes ultimately to find solutions to some of the most common and significant problems faced by families today.

The family conversation

Through the creation of the Centre for the Modern Family, Scottish Widows has committed to adding to the debate around family in two ways. Firstly, by identifying 'New Family Types' based on strong evidence that brings new insights into how we see our families. Secondly, by using the expert voices and interpretation of 'The Panel', whose breadth of opinion reflects the richness and diversity of British society.

To launch this important Centre, Scottish Widows has undertaken a significant research project, asking 3,000 individuals across the UK about their own family make-up and feelings towards it, as well as their views on different family structures in modern society. The headline findings this research has produced show clearly just how much society's attitude to the family has changed in recent years.

Using the detailed demographic and attitudinal data, we have also developed a helpful model for presenting this which provides us with a new, clear way of examining and understanding British families. These 'segments', or New Family Types, have been identified by shared attitudes towards family life, as well as the architecture within individual families.

Our starting point – the traditional Nuclear Family

If you asked a typical British child growing up in the 1960s or 70s to draw their family, you would be very likely to get a picture like this:

It represented the typical British family for most of the last century. But the question the Centre for the Modern Family asked was whether it remained as accurate today?

Not purely in demographic terms, but also in terms of how we view and feel about families. We all know times have changed, but that change is dramatic. People, their lifestyles, wants, needs and social attitudes have changed, and reflecting this, so has their family structure.

In 1961, 38 per cent of families consisted of a married couple with two or more children, the 'traditional model'.[1] Figures published in November 2011, by the Office of National Statistics, show that there continues

1 Office for National Statistics, 'Social Trends 40', (2010 edition), p.14

to be a long-term decline in the proportion of the adult population who are married or widowed, whilst the proportions who are single and divorced continue to rise.[2] The Scottish Widows data shows that today just 16 per cent of the UK population believe that they fit the 'traditional model'. In short, there has been a meltdown in the traditional nuclear family.

So if we fast forward to today, a typical child's sketch of their family might well look very different and could be like this:

And if one type of family looks like this and another type of family looks very different, this raises a number of questions about our society and points to some inherent tensions within it. Can we, and should we, try to reconcile the diverse perspectives on the rights and wrongs of family structure and set up? What can we, as a society, do to meet the needs of these different types of families? Where does the line between tolerance, choice, circumstance and acceptance lie?

June 2012

⇨ The above information is an extract from the Scottish Widows report *Family: Helping to understand the modern British family* and is reprinted with permission. Please visit www.centreformodernfamily.com for further information.

2 Office for National Statistics, Marital Status Population Estimates Excluding Marriages Abroad – Mid 2010

Survey reveals changing understanding of the family unit

The family norm used to be a married couple with two children but a new YouGov survey underscores the increasingly flexible definitions of what constitutes a family today.

When asked what they consider to be a family, almost all those surveyed agreed that a married couple with children fitted this definition.

However, most agree that other set-ups can also be defined as family.

Nearly nine in ten (89%) said an unmarried couple with children counted as a family, followed by a lone parent with at least one child (87%).

Nearly three-quarters (72%) said they would consider a married couple without children as a family, as well as siblings living together (71%).

Over two-thirds (70%) said same-sex couples in civil partnerships with children were a family.

However, the survey found a broader view of family among a sizable group of people who are happy to apply the term 'family' to people who have strong emotional bonds or live together.

More than half (52%) of people consider an unmarried couple without children to be a family, while 47% of people consider a same-sex couple in a civil partnership to be a family.

Over a third (39%) of people consider any two or more people who care for each other to be a family.

Views differed little between religious people and the general population, with 67% of Anglicans, 66% of Catholics and 72% of Jewish people regarding a same-sex couple in a civil partnership with children as a family.

However, the survey suggests most people still prefer a father and a mother for children. When asked whether more single women having children without a male partner is good or bad, 30% said neither but 58% said it was bad.

Views were more mixed when it came to more gay and lesbian couples raising children, with 24% saying this was good, 31% saying bad and 39% saying neither.

The survey also found that although most think churches are welcoming of married and single people, only 45% said they were welcoming to divorced people, and just 21% said they were welcoming to gay, lesbian and bisexual people.

The survey was commissioned by Westminster Faith Debates and asked the views of over 4,000 UK adults.

26 March 2013

⇨ The above information is reprinted with kind permission from Christian Today. Please visit www. christiantoday.com for further information.

Family structure

Key findings: Children's lives are influenced by the number of parents and siblings that they live with, as well as by whether their parents are married. The World Family Map reports these key indicators of family structure in this section of the report.

Although two-parent families are becoming less common in many parts of the world, they still constitute a majority of families around the globe. Children under age 18 are more likely to live in two-parent families than in other family forms in Asia and the Middle East, compared with other regions of the world. Children are more likely to live with one or no parent in the Americas, Europe, Oceania and Sub-Saharan Africa than in other regions.

Extended families (which include parent(s) and kin from outside the nuclear family) also appear to be common in Asia the Middle East, South America and Sub-Saharan Africa, but not in other regions of the world.

Marriage rates are declining in many regions. Adults are most likely to be married in Africa, Asia and the Middle East, and are least likely to be married in South America, with Europe, North America and Oceania falling in between. Cohabitation (living together without marriage) is more common among couples in Europe, North America, Oceania and – especially – in South America.

Childbearing rates are declining worldwide. The highest fertility rates are in Sub-Saharan Africa. A woman gives birth to an average of 5.5 children in Nigeria – down from close to seven in the 1980s, but still high by world standards. Moderate rates of fertility (2.3-3.1) are found in the Middle East, and levels of fertility that are sufficient to replace a country's population in the next generation (about 2.1) are found in the Americas and Oceania. Below replacement-level fertility is found in East Asia and Europe.

Given the decline in marriage rates, childbearing outside of marriage – or nonmarital childbearing – is increasing in many regions.

The highest rates of nonmarital childbearing are found in South America and Europe, paralleling increases in cohabitation, with moderate rates found in North America and Oceania, varied rates found in Sub-Saharan Africa and the lowest rates found in Asia and the Middle East.

Living arrangements

Family living arrangements – how many parents are in the household and whether the household includes extended family members – shape the character and contexts of children's lives, as well as the human resources available for children.

The living arrangements that children experience vary substantially around the globe. Kinship ties are particularly powerful in much of Asia, the Middle East, South America and Sub-Saharan Africa. In the majority of the countries in these regions, more than 40 per cent of children lived in households with other adults besides their parents. In many cases, these adults were extended family members. Indeed, at least half of children lived with adults besides their parents in parts of Africa (Kenya [52 per cent], Nigeria [59 per cent] and South Africa [70 per cent]); Asia (India [50 per cent]); and South America (Nicaragua [55 per cent], Peru [51 per cent] and Colombia [61 per cent]). In these regions, then, children were especially likely to be affected by their relationships with other adults in the household, including grandparents, uncles and cousins, compared with children living in regions where extended household members played smaller roles in children's day-to-day lives.

Whether in nuclear or extended family households, children were especially likely to live with two parents (who could be biological parents or step-parents) in Asia and the Middle East.

On the basis of the data available for the specific countries examined in these regions, more than 80 per cent of children in these three regions lived with two parents (ranging from 84 per cent in Israel/ Turkey to 92 per cent in Jordan). About 80 to 90 per cent of children in European countries lived in two-parent households (ranging from 76 per cent in the United Kingdom to 89 per cent in Italy/Poland). In the Americas, about one-half to three-quarters of children lived in two-parent households, from 53 per cent in Colombia to 78 per cent in Canada. The two-parent pattern was more mixed in Sub-Saharan Africa, ranging from 36 per cent (South Africa) to 69 per cent (Nigeria). Some of these children living in two-parent households were also living with extended families, as noted above.

By contrast, in much of South America and Sub-Saharan Africa, from 16 per cent (Bolivia) to 43 per cent (South Africa) of children lived in single-parent families and from four per cent (Argentina) to 20 per cent (South Africa) of children lived in homes without either of their parents. Among the South American countries in this study, for instance, Colombia had the highest per centage of children living without either of their parents: 12 per cent. The high percentage of South African children living with one parent or without either parent – 43 per cent and 20 per cent, respectively, reflects the high incidence of AIDS orphans,[1] as well as adult mortality from other causes and labour migration.

1   Neddy Rita Matshalaga and Greg Powell, 'Mass Orphanhood in the Era of HIV/AIDS,' British Medical Journal 324 (2002), Anthony J. McMichael et al., 'Mortality Trends and Setbacks: Global Convergence or Divergence,' Lancet 363 (2004).

Finally, although a small percentage of children in North America, Oceania and Europe lived in households without at least one of their parents, a large minority – about one-fifth – lived in single-parent households. Rates were slightly lower in Europe. In these regions, the United States (27 per cent), the United Kingdom (24 per cent) and New Zealand (24 per cent) had particularly high levels of single parenthood. Many European countries have projected the proportion of children living with single parents to grow through 2030.[2]

In short, the regional patterns identified in this section of the *World Family Map* suggest that children are especially likely to live with two parents in Asia and the Middle East. Elsewhere large minorities of children live with either one parent (Europe, North America, Oceania, South America and Sub-Saharan Africa) or neither parent (South America and Sub-Saharan Africa). Extended families are common in Asia, the Middle East, South America and Sub-Saharan Africa.

In general then, extended kinship ties to children appear to be stronger in low-income regions of the world, and children are more likely to live in two-parent families in regions where higher incomes or marriages (see below) are more prevalent.

Marriage and cohabitation

The nature, function and first-hand experience of marriage varies around the world. Marriage looks and feels different in Sweden, compared with the experience in Saudi Arabia; in China, compared with the experience in Canada; and in Argentina, compared with the experience in Australia. Nevertheless, across time and space, in most societies and cultures, marriage has been an important institution for structuring adult intimate relationships and connecting parents to one another and to any children that they have together.[3] In particular, in many countries, marriage has played an important role in providing a stable context for bearing and rearing children, and for integrating fathers into the lives of their children.[4]

However, today the hold of marriage as an institution over the adult life course and the connection between marriage and parenthood vary around much of the globe. Dramatic increases in cohabitation, divorce and nonmarital childbearing in the Americas, Europe and Oceania over the last four decades suggest that the institution of marriage is much less relevant in these parts of the world.[5] At the same time, the meaning of marriage appears to be shifting in much of the world. Marriage is becoming more of an option for adults, rather than a necessity for the survival of adults and children. Cohabitation has emerged an important precursor or alternative to marriage in many countries for any number of reasons. Adults may look for more flexibility or freedom in their relationships, or they may feel that they do not have sufficient financial or emotional resources to marry, or they may perceive marriage as a risky undertaking.[6]

2 Organization for Economic Cooperation and Development (OECD), 'Doing Better for Families,' (OECD, 2011).

3 See, for example, B. Chapais, Primeval Kinship: How Pair Bonding Gave Birth to Human Society (Cambridge, MA: Harvard University Press, 2008), K. Davis, Contemporary Marriage: Comparative Perspectives on a Changing Institution (New York: Russell Sage Foundation, 1985), W. J. Goode, World Revolution and Family Patterns (New York: Free Press, 1963).

4 Chapais, Primeval Kinship: How Pair Bonding Gave Birth to Human Society, P. Heuveline, J. Timberlake, M., and F. F. Furstenberg, 'Shifting Childrearing to Single Mothers: Results from 17 Western Countries', Population and Development Review 29 (2003).

5 R. Lesthaeghe, 'A Century of Demographic and Cultural Change in Western Europe: An Exploration of Underlying Dimensions,' Population and Development Review 9 (1983), P. McDonald, Families in Australia: A Socio-Demographic Perspective (Melbourne: Australian Institute of Family Studies, 1995), D. Popenoe, 'Cohabitation, Marriage, and Child Well-Being: A Cross-National Perspective', (New Brunswick, NJ: The National Marriage Project, 2008).

6 A. Cherlin, The Marriage-Go-Round: The State of Marriage and the Family in America Today (New York: Knopf, 2009), S. Coontz, Marriage: A History: From Obedience to Intimacy or How Love Conquered Marriage (New York: The Penguin Group, 2005), W. J. Goode, World Change in Divorce Patterns (New Haven, CT: Yale University Press, 1993), Heuveline, Timberlake, and Furstenberg, 'Shifting Childrearing to Single Mothers: Results from 17 Western Countries.'

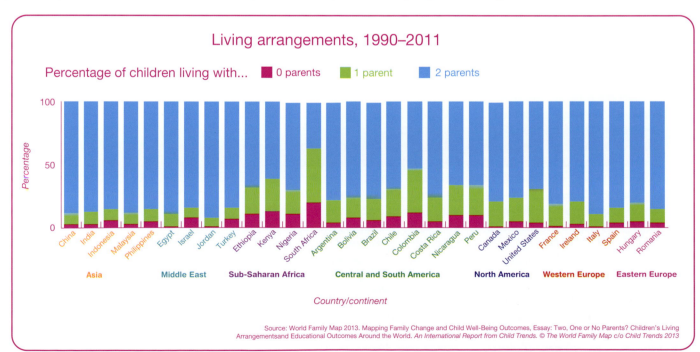

Living arrangements, 1990–2011

Percentage of children living with... ■ 0 parents ■ 1 parent ■ 2 parents

Source: World Family Map 2013. Mapping Family Change and Child Well-Being Outcomes, Essay: Two, One or No Parents? Children's Living Arrangements and Educational Outcomes Around the World. *An International Report from Child Trends.* © The World Family Map c/o Child Trends 2013

Given the changing patterns and perceptions about marriage and cohabitation in many contemporary societies, this section from the *World Family Map* measures how prevalent marriage and cohabitation are among adults in their prime childbearing and childrearing years (18–49) around the globe.

Data indicates that adults aged 18–49 were most likely to be married in Africa, Asia and the Middle East, and were least likely to be married in South America. Marriage levels fell in the moderate range (about half) in most of Europe, Oceania and North America. Moreover, the data show that a larger percentage of adults were cohabiting in Europe, the Americas and Oceania than in other regions.

Between 47 (Singapore) and 77 per cent (India) of the young adult population in the Asian countries included in this report were married, and marriage was even more common in the Middle East, where a clear majority of adults (between 61 [Turkey] and 80 [Egypt] per cent) were married.

By contrast, marriage patterns fell in the mid-range, or were less consistent, in the Americas, Europe and Sub-Saharan Africa. In North America and Oceania, about half of adults aged 18-49 were married, ranging from 43 (Canada) to 58 per cent (Mexico). In the Sub-Saharan African countries studied, marriage patterns showed a great deal of variation, with between 30 (South Africa) and 67 per cent (Nigeria) of adults aged 18–49 married. Indeed, South Africa had one of the lowest marriage levels of any country included in this study. Likewise, among the European countries, between 37 (Sweden) and 60 per cent (Romania) of adults aged 18–49 were married, with marriage clearly being more common in Eastern Europe. By contrast, in South America, generally, less than 40 per cent of adults were married; in Colombia, the proportion of married adults in that age group was a low 19 per cent.

Data indicates that cohabitation was rare in Asia and the Middle East, two regions where relatively

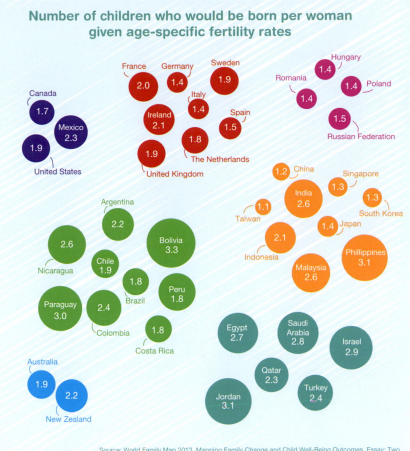

Number of children who would be born per woman given age-specific fertility rates

Source: World Family Map 2013. Mapping Family Change and Child Well-Being Outcomes, Essay: Two, One or No Parents? Children's Living Arrangements and Educational Outcomes Around the World. *An International Report from Child Trends. © The World Family Map c/o Child Trends 2013*

traditional mores still dominate family life. Moderate to high levels of cohabitation were found in North America and Oceania, where between eight (Mexico/United States) and 19 per cent (Canada) of adults aged 18–49 were in cohabiting relationships. Levels of cohabitation in Sub-Saharan Africa varied considerably, with comparatively high levels of cohabitation in South Africa (13 per cent) and low levels in Ethiopia (four per cent), Nigeria (two per cent) and Kenya (4 per cent).

The data also show high levels of cohabitation in much of Europe. For example about one-quarter of Swedish and French adults aged 18–49 were living in a cohabiting relationship. Cohabitation is most common among South Americans, where consensual unions have played a longstanding role in South American society. Between 12 (Chile) and 39 per cent (Colombia) of adults aged 18–49 lived in cohabiting unions in South America, with Colombia registering the highest level of cohabitation of any country in our global study.

In general, marriage seems to be more common in Asia and the Middle East, whereas alternatives to marriage – including cohabitation – were more common in Europe and South America. North America, Oceania and Sub-Saharan Africa fell in between. Both cultural and economic forces may help to account for these regional differences.

It remains to be seen, however, how the varied place of marriage in society – and the increasing popularity of cohabitation in many regions of the world – affect the well-being of children in countries around the globe.

⇨ The above information is an extract from the *World Family Map 2013* report from Child Trends and is reprinted with permission. Please visit www.worldfamilymap.org for further information.

© The World Family Map c/o Child Trends 2013

The Symmetrical Family

By Richard Reeves

Let's dispense with the clichés up front: strong families are a vital foundation of a good society; family life is changing significantly; children are our most precious citizens.

So far, so obvious. But which institution, or institutions, are we talking about here? The last Labour Government reportedly spent weeks on an internal argument over whether a green paper should refer to 'the family' at all or simply to 'families'. There is some substance behind these semantics. 'The Family' – capital T, capital F – denotes, for many, a husband and wife plus a couple of kids, with perhaps a distinct nod towards roles for the parents: breadwinning for Dad, childrearing for Mum.

By contrast, 'families' provides a broader canvas. There are single parent families, cohabiting families, gay families, step-families. So by using 'families' rather than The Family, we hope to avoid passing judgement.

I think it is time to stop fretting about this, not least because some unappealing labels can get generated. For a while, policy wonks talked about 'reconstituted families', which sound as appealing as reconstituted meat.

A family is a household in which children are being raised. By one parent or two. Gay or straight. Natural, adoptive or step. Married, remarried, widowed or cohabiting. The rainbow of possible family types is simply greater today than at most other points in history. The title of a hit TV series *Modern Family* sums up the trend.

To say that families are modern is not of course to say that all modern families are equal. They are certainly not doing an equally good job of raising the next generation. And some of the inequalities relate to some of the structural factors, although not in a straightforward way.

Calling for a restoration of The Family, or of 'traditional family life', is like wishing people back into the pews on Sundays. It is pointless in two senses. First, because there are no real levers to make it happen: you are merely shouting into the wind.

Second, because it misses the point. Improving the quality of family life in all its rainbow of options, and in particular the quality of parenting, is the point. The particular structure of the family is an important question, but a second-order one.

The argument that follows is in three parts. First, I describe the principal changes that have occurred in family life in the last 30 years, since the foundation of 4Children. The

main trends are well known: smaller families; older parents; higher rates of divorce, cohabitation and single parenthood; and greater labour market participation by mothers.

The changes of the last three decades represent the latest stage in the transformation of the family from an economic institution to a social one – and therefore from one based, in part at least, on financial necessity to one based on individual choice. In the past, the family has played an important role in economic production and distribution. Today, in the era of the welfare state and high women's employment, the principal role of the family is the socialisation, education and care of children. Of course the family has performed this social function in the past, and of course the family still plays an economic role today. But the balance has shifted decisively. Many of the changes of the last 30 years have to be seen in this light.

Second, I set out the main opportunities and challenges for families today. Again, there are few surprises here. Balancing the desire of adults to be in satisfying relationships with the need of children for stable parenting. The decline of marriage. The trials of young men apparently left without a clear familial role: men who are seen as 'redundant' in the full sense of the term. The struggles of single mothers to raise their children well. The challenge for lower and middle-income families of paying the bills, while paying enough attention to the children and to each other. Expensive and/or poor quality childcare. Stagnant real wages in middle and lower-income families, along with austerity-generated cuts in tax credits and other benefits. And, in a sense most worrying of all, an increasing gap in the life chances of children emerging from the most successful and the least successful families. On the other hand, we now see vastly expanded opportunities for women; a better education system, including new pre-school education;

a narrowing of the gender pay gap; much greater involvement by most fathers in their children's lives; a proper focus on domestic violence; greater flexibility in the workplace; high levels of satisfaction with family life; and greater equality for same-sex couples and parents.

Third, I will set out an agenda for the next 30 years. We are half-way through a revolution in the interaction between gender roles and family life. I will argue that we have to keep going, and see similar changes in men's lives to the ones we have seen for women. While some yearn for a return to 'The Family', I will argue that there is no turning back. Even if it were possible, which I believe it is not, it would not be desirable. We live in a modern liberal society, where both women and men rightly seek greater choices and more opportunities.

Greater equality between men and women is a fact of modern life, and we should be further narrowing the gap, not seeking to widen it again. But we also want to find ways to make family life more sustainable, and more conducive to effective childrearing. If families are not to act as automatic transmitters of inequality, then we need to find ways to help poorer families keep up with the more affluent, especially in the parenting race. One way to do all of this is to realise the vision of Michael Young and Peter Willmott in their book *The Symmetrical Family*. A family in which men and women can share, on equal terms, in the joint tasks of breadwinning and childrearing.

I will argue that the asymmetry in current family life reinforced by law, culture and custom – is at the root of many of our family problems. At every level of society, greater gender equality will underpin better family life. If, and it is a big if, men are up to it.

By 2043, if we are successful, the terms 'career woman', 'working father' or 'stay-at-home Dad' will have lost their novelty. Gender equality is good for everyone. It is good for women, for children, and yes, even for men. And it is vital for restoring balance, but equal balance, to family life. The Symmetrical Family is obviously fairer. But the Symmetrical Family will be more sustainable too.

⇨ The above information is an extract from *The Symmetrical Family* and is reprinted with kind permission from 4Children. Please visit www.4children. org.uk for further information.

Families in 2020 – what support will they need?

What will families look like in 2020? How can we best describe and predict their needs? And how can we work to best equip them for the challenges ahead?

On 30 November, 2009, our Chief Executive Dr Katherine Rake began to develop FPI's focus on future families with a speech in Westminster.

Dr Rake argued that we need to fundamentally broaden our understanding of the UK family in order to meet its needs for 2020.

She said: 'Our current understanding of the family as centred on the parent-child relationship will be augmented as we understand more about how the adult couple and the relationship between the child and the whole family – grandparents, step-parents, aunts, uncles and siblings – can play a critical role in securing a child's well-being.'

Dr Rake also spoke of the implications of the UK's ageing population, and the changes in the nature of UK fatherhood.

What can we learn from families in Finland?

Scandanavian nations are frequently cited for their forward-thinking approaches to supporting family life – including generous parental leave and universal childcare and daycare. The UK's status as a family-friendly society pales in comparison.

New mothers can even receive a state maternity package of baby clothes.

Katja Forssén, a Professor of Social Work at the University of Turku, Finland, shared with the Family and Parenting Institute the lessons the UK can learn from the country. See her presentation, Family policy: the Finnish experience at http://www.familyandparenting. org/Resources/FPI/Documents/Conf09KatjaForssen. pdf.

⇨ The above information is reprinted with kind permission from the Family and Childcare Trust. Please visit www.familyandchildcaretrust.org for further information.

Which type of modern family are you?

Society is changing significantly, and much of that change is being driven by people's family lives.

The Centre for the Modern Family's research has allowed us to divide up the population into ten distinct groups, based on people's common characteristics, attitudes and experiences. The members of each group have a unique set of dimensions in common, but which differ from other groupings.

This rich and insightful segmentation has long-term relevance in understanding people's attitudes and behaviours, enabling us to understand the challenges they face and the support they need.

Onederfuls

Young, single and with few close family relationships, this group is happy with their family set-up, but feels poorly portrayed by the media.

Segment overview

People in this segment tend to be younger, with a high proportion of under-24s. They are more likely to be single and slightly more likely to be male. They all come from varied family set-ups and many of them report few close family relationships with limited contact and lack of a family member

to whom they can turn for advice and support.

Their attitudes towards a range of family structures are positive and their limited family closeness doesn't bother them. Nevertheless some of them still feel judged because of their family network and most feel their situation is not well portrayed in the media.

Modern Classics

Unlike their parents, this group believes that society is moving away from 'the 2.4 children family', but still have a more traditional family structure themselves.

Segment overview

This segment is younger and most open to a broad variety of family structures. Most are of white British background and many are living comfortably on their income, with almost half working full time.

They tend to feel their own family set-up is typical and sufficiently valued by society. Although relatively close to their family, their differing views on family networks can cause friction. They are less likely to share the same values, or to say they think about family in a similar way to their parents, and only some desire greater closeness.

Born and Red

This group believes that the family is changing and, like their parents, are very open in their views about what a family should be.

Segment overview

This segment pre-dominantly consists of younger people under 45. Most are of white British background and from social grade ABC1. Many are married, and men and women in this segment are also likely to be cohabiting.

The vast majority feel very close to their family. They are particularly close to their parents with whom they share common values.

Although they feel their own family set-up is typical, they are very open in their views of what a 'proper family' should be, particularly concerning same-sex couples and single parents. The majority also believe that society will think about family in a different way in the future.

Middletowners

Usually affluent, they are close to their family, feel well catered for and do not think that society is out of date with its view of families in Britain today.

Segment overview

People in this segment are more likely to be affluent, white and from ABC1 social grades. They have close family relationships, particularly with their parents, and share their values.

They feel their family set-up is typical or fairly typical and well catered for by government and business, as well as portrayed in the media. Hardly any of them believe that society's view of the family is out of date or that people will think about family in a very different way in the future.

Although they are accepting of single, cohabiting and divorced family set-ups they are likely to believe that the term 2.4 children still applies today.

Deconstruction Workers

Likely to be middle-aged divorcees, who are coping well with the pressures that this brings, but feel that society does not cater for their family set-up.

Segment overview

People in this segment tend to be middle-aged, with almost half in their late 40s or early 50s. They tend to have more experience of divorce than average, leaving some as either single parents or living away from their kids.

Either way, many have financial commitments to more than one family. They tend to think their family values are different from others in their family although most are unconcerned about this. In general they have more permissive attitudes towards alternative family set-ups. Some would openly say that society is out of date in its view of the modern family. All feel that their own family type is not valued enough by society and many feel they are not catered for by government or businesses.

New Traditionalists

Made up mainly of ethnic minorities, this group places a strong emphasis on cultural heritage, marriage and close-knit family relationships.

Segment overview

Over half the people in this segment are married and there is a very low rate of divorce. A high proportion are from a non-white background and they tend to be less affluent, with almost one-third from social grade DE.

Almost all in this segment are religious, with their beliefs playing an important role in their lives. Shared family values are very important to them and they tend to have very traditional views about the family, believing strongly in the importance of marriage and with a higher incidence of negative attitudes towards same-sex couples than any other group.

Although many have grown up outside the UK, they believe it is important for family members to live close to one another.

Groan Ups

Mainly made up of older generations, this segment has a traditional outlook on the family and its role. Whilst they feel typical, they also believe that society is increasingly ignoring 'the 2.4 children family'.

Segment overview

This is an older segment with traditional values. Most people in this segment are married and are parents, although in most cases their children will have left home.

They are close to their spouse and in general, close family relationships and shared values are important to them, as is regular contact with family members living outside their home. Religion is likely to play an

important role in their lives, which may partly account for their traditional attitudes and belief in the importance of marriage. But while most of them feel their family set-up is typical, almost everyone in this segment feels undervalued by society and not well catered for by government or the media.

Once Upon a Timers

Strong supporters of traditional family models, they are younger and many are from ethnic minorities, religious and close-knit families. This group emphasises the importance of marriage in making a proper family, but believes that society undervalues this.

Segment overview

People in this segment tend to be younger, with a high proportion of 25–34s. They come from close-knit families and have a traditional view of what makes a family.

Many have grown up in another country and almost a third of them say that their religious beliefs influence how they live their lives a great deal. They tend to think that modern family types are not 'proper' families. This applies particularly to same-sex couples, single-parent families and families with unmarried parents. They can feel judged because of their own

family set-up and most are not happy with the way their family are portrayed in the media.

Old Loud and Prouds

Mainly retired, this group are coping well financially and feel valued by society. They hold traditional views which are shared by their families.

Segment overview

People in this segment tend to be over 65 and the majority are retired. They have very traditional values, which may be partly influenced by their religious beliefs as well as their age. It is important to them that their family shares similar values.

They tend to live in two-person households but some live alone. Overall, they seem to be contented. They tend to feel happy with their level of involvement with their family, valued by society and many are living comfortably within their means.

⇨ The above information is reprinted with kind permission from the Centre for the Modern Family. Please visit www. centreformodernfamily.com for further information.

© Centre for Modern Family 2013

Key facts on parenthood

⇨ Numbers of live births have risen substantially in England over the past decade, from just over 600,000 births in the year 2000 to 700,000 in 2009. In the past year, rates have risen by 2.4%, from just over 706,248 in 2009 to 723,165 in 2010. (Source: Office for National Statistics, 2011)

⇨ London has the highest birth rate in England (defined as the number of live births per 1,000 women aged 15 to 44). (Source: ONS, 2011)

⇨ The lowest conception rate in England was in the North-East at just 73.1 conceptions per 1,000 women. This region also had the lowest birth rate at 60.2 births per 1,000 women aged 15–44 years. (Source: ONS, 2011)

⇨ The United Kingdom has one of the highest Total Fertility Rates of all the European countries at 2.0 children per woman. (Source: World Health Organization, 2010)

⇨ Most babies in 2009 were born to women aged between 30–34, with 202,457 births. (Source: ONS, 2011)

⇨ Mothers have got older. The average age of a mother in 1971 was 26.6, and this had risen to 29.3 in 2008. By age group, the highest numbers of births were by women in their early 20s in 1971. This had changed to their late 20s and early 30s by 2009. In contrast, the number of women having babies before age 20 has halved. (Source: ONS, 2011)

⇨ Women having babies in their late 30s has more than doubled from 45.2 births to 114.3 births per 1,000. The number of women having babies after the age 40 has also doubled since 1971, from 12.7 to 27 in 1,000 births. (Source: ONS, 2011)

⇨ Far fewer babies are being born to married couples. The number of babies born outside marriage increased sixfold over the past 40 years. Most babies born in 1971 (92%) were to married couples, but in 2010 this fell to about half that (53%). This change is closely associated with fewer marriages, more divorces and a shift to unmarried couples living together instead. (Source: ONS, 2011)

⇨ There has been a large decline in the number of adoptions with only 4,550 in 2010 across all age groups, compared with 22,502 in 1974. (Source: ONS, 2011)

⇨ Conception rates in England and Wales dipped around the turn of the century, but have risen and returned to the levels observed in the early 1990s. In 2001, among every 1,000 women aged 15–44 years there were around 70 conceptions; in 2009 there were just over 80. (Source: ONS, 2011)

⇨ The number of births occurring by in vitro fertilisation (IVF) in England has increased significantly since use of the technique became more accepted: from 1,226 IVF babies in 1991 to 5,935 in 2005. (Source: Human Fertilisation Embryology Authority, 2007)

⇨ The above information is reprinted with kind permission from OnePlusOne. Please visit www.oneplusone.org.uk for further information.

Lone parents tally heads for two million as numbers rise 20,000 a year, says Centre for Social Justice report

⇨ Around one million children grow up with no contact with their father

⇨ Many are in 'men deserts' and have no male role model in sight

⇨ Prime Minister urged to get a grip and finally deliver on his pledge to tackle family breakdown

⇨ The tragedy of family break-up is devastating children, parents and communities

Lone parent families are increasing at a rate of more than 20,000 a year and will total more than two million by the time of the next election, according to a major new report accusing the Government of turning a blind eye to its commitment to promote family stability.

The report, to be published in full this week (w/c 10 June), also finds that at least one million children are growing up without a father and that some of the poorest parts of the country have become 'men deserts' because so few primary schools have male teachers.

Across England one in four state primary schools have no full-time qualified male teacher, and 80 per cent of state-educated boys are in primary schools with three or fewer full-time qualified male teachers.[1]

Father absence is linked to higher rates of teenage crime, pregnancy and disadvantage, the report warns.

In a foreword to the report, titled: *'Fractured Families: why stability matters'*, from the Centre for Social Justice (CSJ), Director Christian Guy warns of the 'tsunami' of family breakdown battering the country.

[1] Amended at 10.30am on 17.06.13 from 'Across England and Wales, one in four primary schools has no male teacher and 80 per cent have fewer than three.'

He says the human, social and financial costs are 'devastating' for children and adults alike. Yet faced with this national 'emergency', the response from politicians of the Left and the Right has been 'feeble'. Mr Guy comments: 'There are many misguided reasons for such political paralysis. Some argue that it is no business of politicians to meddle in the personal family choices people make. Others suggest that rising family breakdown is just a modern process, an inevitable trait of human advancement. Others say family instability doesn't matter...

'This has to change. Our political discourse about family policy must mature. Family breakdown is an urgent public health issue. Backing commitment and setting a goal of reducing instability does not equate to criticising or stigmatising lone parents or those involved.

'Within this need for new maturity, we should also agree that marriage is not a right-wing obsession but a social justice issue: people throughout society want to marry but the cultural and financial barriers faced by those in the poorest communities thwart their aspirations.'

The report features 'league tables' showing the parts of the country (Lower Layer Super Output Areas, which have an average population of 1,614) where fatherless and lone parent households are most prevalent.

In one neighbourhood in the Riverside ward of Liverpool, there is no father present in 65 per cent of households with dependent children. Liverpool has eight out of the country's top 20 areas with the highest levels of fatherless households.

There are 236 LSOAs in England and Wales where more than 50 per cent of households with dependent children are headed by a lone mother.

An area in the Manor Castle ward of Sheffield tops the lone parent league table – among households with dependent children, 75 per cent are headed by a lone parent (most commonly a woman). Second comes the same Riverside neighbourhood in Liverpool (71 per cent). Five Liverpool neighbourhoods are in the top 20 nationally for lone parent households.

Mr Guy adds: 'For children growing up in some of the poorest parts of the country, men are rarely encountered in the home or in the classroom. This is an ignored form of deprivation that can have profoundly damaging consequences on social and mental development.

'There are "men deserts" in many parts of our towns and cities and we urgently need to wake up to what is going wrong.' The CSJ report recalls David Cameron's election pledge to lead the 'most family-friendly Government ever'. Yet, in power, the family stability agenda 'has barely been mentioned'. Comprehensive action to tackle existing policy barriers to family stability 'has been almost entirely absent', it adds.

The report also highlights the cost to the taxpayer of soaring rates of family breakdown. The total cost is estimated at £46 billion a year or £1,541 for every taxpayer in the country. This figure has risen by nearly a quarter in the last four years and on current trends, the cost of family breakdown is projected to hit £49 billion by the end of this Parliament.

The CSJ report condemns the lack of Government action to stem the epidemic of family breakdown. For every £6,000 spent on picking up the pieces after a split, just £1 is spent on helping to keep families together.

The research also finds that it is the instability of cohabiting couples rather than a surge in divorce rates that is fuelling the disintegration of the UK family. Since 1996, the number of people cohabiting has doubled to nearly six million.

Cohabiting parents are three times more likely to separate by the time a child is aged five than married couples, the report states.

The high break-up rates among cohabiting couples are driving up the numbers of lone parents. These increased by almost a quarter between 1996 and 2012 and now account for nearly two million adults, mostly women. One quarter of all families with dependent children are now headed by a lone parent as Britain experiences one of the highest rates of family breakdown in the developed world.

The report also highlights how family breakdown is causing additional strain on housing markets; both in social housing – where availability is already stretched – and private housing.

On the Government's troubled families scheme, the report criticises the deadline of 2015 as arbitrary and calls for a longer term cross-party commitment to be reached on helping these families. It also states that the process for identifying families has been poor and a CSJ FoI request revealed that less than 16.5 per cent of all the families identified so far meet all three of the set criteria of youth crime or anti-social behaviour, truanting and an adult on out-of-work benefits.

17 June 2013

⇨ The above information is reprinted with kind permission from The Centre for Social Justice. Please visit www.centreforsocialjustice.org.uk for further information.

Changing families

How children are affected when parents separate and how to support them.

If parents separate, their children are likely to be affected. It's important for everyone – parents, grandparents and any new partners involved – to keep the needs of the children uppermost in their minds.

The importance of maintaining contact

If parents separate, one parent may move away or start a new relationship/family. In some circumstances, a parent may block a child's contact with the other parent, grandparents or other family members. Sometimes a parent will choose to break off contact with their children. In these circumstances children are likely to have trouble maintaining contact with both parents.

There is strong evidence that in almost every situation, it's in the child's best interests to maintain contact with both of their parents – and their grandparents too. Having a healthy relationship with both parents contributes to children's emotional well-being.

The effects of changes to living arrangements

After a separation some children may have to relocate to a new area. They may have to leave their school and friends behind.

If a parent's new partner moves in, children may resent the absence of the parent who no longer lives at home; they may feel that their position or role in the family is threatened by the arrival of a new adult or child; or they may have problems with how the new adult approaches family life and parenting.

Emotional needs of children

Separation can cause children to suffer emotions like sadness, guilt and frustration. Therefore, it's important to give your child plenty of support by talking to them and listening to what they have to say.

Although it's something that no one likes to think about, there is also a chance that your child will be put at risk as a result of a new relationship. It's important to take things slowly and be absolutely sure of the right way to move on. After all, your child's emotional and physical well-being should be your first concern.

Supporting children through change

If your family is moving on, you can help to protect your child and support them.

Keep talking to your ex, it will help your children to maintain contact. Don't put your ex down, and if you can, show that you are still parenting together.

Talk to your children about what is happening and listen to what they have to say.

Try to maintain the normal routine during difficult times.

Give your children time to adjust and take things slowly. Let your new partner know your rules. They should take your lead, especially in matters of discipline. If your child is living with your ex's new partner, it's normal to feel concerned, but give the new partner time and space to adjust.

An ongoing relationship with both parents is best for a child.

⇨ The above information is reprinted with kind permission from the NSPCC. Please visit www.nspcc.org.uk for further information.

What your child may feel when you separate

The better you understand how your child is feeling, the easier it will be for your to make your relationship with them positive and secure.

When parents live apart or the family separates, this can be a very difficult time for children. They can feel:

⇨ Confused

⇨ Frightened

⇨ Sad

⇨ Hurt

⇨ Rejected

⇨ Betrayed

⇨ Angry

⇨ Guilty.

Try to understand what your child is thinking and feeling. This will allow you to help them adjust better and make sure their needs are not forgotten.

How will I know if my child is stressed or anxious?

It can be quite hard to spot signs of emotional distress in children.

The signs will vary depending on the age of the child.

Here are some of the ways your separation might affect your child:

Babies

Parents can pass on their anger or depression to babies at a vital time in their growth.

Try to give your baby plenty of cuddles, smiles and good eye contact.

Aged two to five

Your child may be more angry, tearful or sad.

Boys may become restless, withdrawn or disruptive; girls may try to become 'little adults' to take care of either parent.

Look out for behaviour that had stopped some time ago, such as bedwetting.

Aged six to eight

Feeling rejected and unloved. You may notice a drop in school performance or hear that they have become disruptive in class.

Boys will very often miss their fathers a lot more than girls will.

Aged nine to 11

Often become very angry, especially towards the parent that they blame for the separation.

They often feel frightened and just want you to get back together again.

You may notice an increase in headaches, sickness or nightmares.

Older children

May become more independent and focus their energies outside the family while the parents are dealing with their own feelings and problems.

They may drift away from the family and look for approval from their friends.

⇨ The above information is reprinted with kind permission from the Child Maintenance and Enforcement Commission. Please visit www.cmoptions.org for further information.

Different Families

A report from Stonewall examining the experiences of children with lesbian and gay parents.

There's no such thing as a typical family. What makes a family differs from child to child. Some children have a mum and a dad, some live with just their mum or just their dad, or with grandparents, or uncles and aunts, or foster parents or carers. Some children have two mums or two dads. Or some have two mums, a dad and grandparents. Families come in lots of different shapes and sizes. The children who talked to us come from lots of different sorts of families too. Some are described on this page.

Josh's (12) family

12-year-old Josh lives in the Midlands with his mum and his dog, Spot. Josh's mum and dad were together, but Josh's dad left when he was very young. Josh's older sister has moved out. He sees his sister regularly, but doesn't see his father. Josh's mother came out to Josh as a lesbian a couple of years ago when he was ten. Josh enjoys school and has a good group of friends there. He enjoys playing Xbox with his friends, going bowling and going to Scouts.

Anya (16) and Glynn's (14) family

16-year-old Anya's birth parents are her father, Alistair, who's gay, and her heterosexual mother, Amy. Alistair and Amy were friends who decided to have a child together. Amy married John shortly after and had Anya's brother, Glynn, who is now 14. Anya considers herself to have four parents as does Glynn, though he's not biologically related to Alistair or his long-term partner, Roger.

Anya and Glynn live in Wales with Amy and John, but regularly stay with dads Alistair and Roger as well. As Anya and Glynn get older however, friends, school and part-time jobs cut into time spent with the family. Glynn plays rugby, enjoys cooking and has his friends round to spend time with him at both his homes. Anya is now in college, has a part-time job and is mainly hanging out with friends, but generally sees her father and his side of the family on Sundays when they have a meal or go to the cinema.

Alice (7) and Hannah's (16) family

Hannah is 16. Her mum was married to her father, but Hannah's parents separated when she was two. Hannah lived with just her mother, Sarah, until Sarah met her current partner, Jo. Sarah, a teacher, and Jo, a civil servant, have always been open as a couple in their small northern town and have never had any problems. Sarah and Jo then had Alice, now age seven. Alice was conceived via anonymous sperm donor to biological mother Sarah.

Hannah sees her father once every three weeks. Hannah sees her biological parents as her parents, and her mother and father's partners as stepmothers. Hannah tends to go to Jo with practical problems, like problems within a friendship group, but to her mother for emotional guidance, such as issues with her father or a boyfriend. Hannah is currently in a sixth-form college.

Alice likes to do art with her mother, Sarah, and rides her bicycle and goes jogging with Jo. Alice calls both Sarah and Jo mummy. Alice likes spelling and science, playing chase and football at playtime, but doesn't like times tables. Outside school, Alice goes to singing and keyboard lessons. When Alice grows up, she'd like to first be a pop star, then a famous doctor, next a famous inventor and then to run in the Olympics.

Mark's (8) family

Mark, eight, lives in London and is the only child of mums Kate and Di, but is surrounded with aunts, uncles, cousins and grandparents. Mark is top of his class in maths, reading and spelling. Mark doesn't really like playtime anymore, because some of his good friends have left the school, but does enjoy playing football. At home, when not cooking with his mums, he enjoys watching Willie Wonka 'over and over and over again'.

Key findings from the *Different Families* report by Stonewall

How I feel about my family

⇨ Many children of gay parents see their families as special and different because all families are special and different though some feel that their families are a lot closer than other people's families.

⇨ Some children feel that their family is a bit different if they have lesbian or gay parents but this is something to celebrate, not worry about.

⇨ Other children do recognise that children with gay parents are less common than other sorts of families, but don't feel this means that their families are any different to other people's families because of it.

⇨ Very young children don't think their families are different from other people's families at all.

How other people feel about my family

Most people, including friends at school, are fine about children having gay parents. They think it is a good thing, or don't really care.

When children are younger though they can be a bit confused and don't understand that someone can have two mums or two dads because their family isn't like that. This means they sometimes have lots of questions for children who have gay parents.

Sometimes other children can be mean about gay people because they have never met any gay people and don't know much about them.

Some people make judgements about what it's like to have gay parents. They think children will have a certain type of life and not as good an upbringing. Children with gay parents can find these judgements upsetting.

Children with gay parents like having gay parents and wouldn't want things to change but wish other people were more accepting.

My experience at school

Children with gay parents don't like the way the word 'gay' is used as an insult in primary and secondary school. Some children said they try and stop people using the word in this way, but find it difficult.

Children say that teachers think the word 'gay' is a bit like a swear word and they don't respond to anti-gay language in the same way they respond to racist language.

Even when children with gay parents are very young they have to answer lots of questions from their friends about their family. This makes them feel unusual.

Once people understand, the questions stop but they start again when children move to different classes or schools.

Some children with gay parents find it easy to answer these questions, but others find it annoying and uncomfortable.

Some of the children are worried about bullying – especially when they first go to secondary school but many children with gay parents haven't experienced any bullying because their parents are gay.

But when children in primary and secondary school do experience bullying to do with having gay parents, schools aren't always very good at doing anything about it.

Children with gay parents said that lesbian, gay or bisexual people or families are never mentioned in schools and they find this difficult and it makes them feel invisible.

Sometimes this means they don't tell people they have gay parents. They are worried about what may happen if other children know they have gay parents. This is stressful and they wish they could tell other people about their families.

Children with gay parents want their schools to talk about different families and stop homophobic bullying. This would make them feel more able to be themselves in school.

⇨ The above information is reprinted with kind permission from Stonewall. Please visit www.stonewall.org.uk for further information, or to read the *Different Families* report in full.

That's mum and mum, me with dad and my other mum.

Same-sex parents 'should be featured in school books'

Children's books used in primary schools should feature same-sex parents to help teach tolerance among youngsters, according to an academic.

By Graeme Paton

Mark McGlashan, from Lancaster University, said pupils as young as five should be introduced to texts that 'challenge homophobic bullying and encourage inclusivity in schools'.

There is evidence that giving young children access to picture books that show gay and lesbian characters in a good light can have 'positive benefits' and promote equality, it is claimed.

His comments come before a conference in Westminster next week aimed at understanding how homophobia and homophobic bullying can be challenged through the use of resources in primary schools.

Earlier this year, the National Union of Teachers urged staff to use 'anti-sexist' materials designed to challenge common gender stereotypes.

The union has designed lessons using such books that are being used in schools in Norfolk, Portsmouth, London and Nottingham. It recommends books such as *Bill's New Frock*, *The Boy With Pink Hair*, *William's Doll*, *The Different Dragon*, *Girls Are Best* and *Dogs Don't Do Ballet*.

Last week, Michael Gove, the Education Secretary, also called for fresh action to stamp out the use of the word 'gay' as an insult in schools.

Mr McGlashan, who has done extensive analyses of representations of same-sex parents in picture books, said next week's conference would 'look at children's literature as a means to challenge homophobic bullying and encourage inclusivity in schools'.

'Part of that aim could include increasing the availability of LGBT literature to educators,' he said.

'There is evidence that promoting cultural inclusivity in early years education has positive benefits with regard to challenging homophobia and this will also be discussed at the conference.

'Research has shown that resources such as picture books can be positively implemented in primary schools to tackle homophobia at its roots.

'Ofsted now specifically looks at homophobic bullying as an issue in schools and it really is a significant problem.

'The idea is that LGBT-inclusive literature could help schools address an issue that really is negatively impacting the lives of young people but the resources aren't there – there just isn't enough good literature available.'

The event, which will be attended by academic experts, publishers and politicians, including Stephen Twigg, Labour's shadow education secretary, aims to generate debate on how literature featuring same-sex parents can be used to break down prejudices and challenge stereotypes prevalent in schools.

The conference – funded by Lancaster's Faculty of Arts and Social Sciences (FASS) Enterprise Centre – will be held on 16 July at Westminster Hall.

The event has also been created in association with Lancaster's Centre for Corpus Approaches to Social Science (CASS), funded by the Economic and Social Research Council (ESRC).

Mr McGlashan said: 'The consultation should result in the production of a number of recommendations to make better quality resources available to educators.

'Bringing together people to discuss the need to grow the LGBT-inclusive children's literature market, we hope will address some of the shortfalls that exist and produce a number of recommendations for the use of these books in schools as well as discuss their status in retail.'

He added: 'Homophobic bullying in schools is a significant and prevalent issue. A Stonewall report in 2012 revealed 55 per cent of LGB children in British schools experience bullying.

'Children's literature is a key educational source in creating an inclusive culture. LGBT-inclusive books are yet to become a staple of school libraries.

'But, why not integrate or produce LGBT-inclusive resources that help our schools prevent homophobic bullying? There is work in the area but not enough and this is what this conference is hoping to address.

'There is a growing recognition of the need, want and support for resources aimed at young people to promote inclusive, anti-homophobic practices but there is still little being done to address the lack of resources.'

10 July 2013

⇨ The above information is reprinted with kind permission from *The Telegraph*. Please visit www.telegraph.co.uk for further information.

© Graeme Paton/The Telegraph 2013

I've got two dads – and they adopted me

Research into adoptive families headed by same-sex couples paints a positive picture of relationships and well-being in these new families. The study, which was carried out by Cambridge University, suggests that adoptive families with gay fathers might be faring particularly well.

In-depth research into the experiences of adoptive families headed by same-sex couples suggests that children adopted by gay or lesbian couples are just as likely to thrive as those adopted by heterosexual couples. It also reveals that new families cope just as well as traditional families with the big challenges that come with taking on children who have had a poor start in life.

A report outlining key findings from the research – which was carried out by a team at Cambridge University's Centre for Family Research – is published today by the British Association of Adoption and Fostering (BAAF) to coincide with LGBT Adoption and Fostering Week. The study is the first of its kind in the UK.

The research explored in considerable detail the experiences of 130 adoptive families, looking at important aspects of family relationships, parental well-being and child adjustment. The study compared three kinds of adoptive families: those headed by gay fathers

(41 families), those headed by lesbian mothers (40 families), and those headed by heterosexual parents (49 families).

'We worked with more than 70 adoption agencies across the UK to recruit families. The participating families were similar in terms of ethnicity, socioeconomic status and education,' says Professor Susan Golombok, director of the Centre for Family Research and co-author of the report.

'Overall we found markedly more similarities than differences in experiences between family types. The differences that did emerge relate to levels of depressive symptoms in parents, which are especially low for gay fathers, and the contrasting pathways to adoption which was second choice for many of the heterosexual and some lesbian parents – but first choice for all but one of the gay parents.'

The study took the form of home visits to the families, written questionnaires and recorded parent-child play sessions. All but four of the children studied were aged between four and eight years old, and all had been placed in their families for at least 12 months prior to being interviewed. All families had two parents.

Each year adoptive families are needed for some 4,000 children. Same-sex couples have had the legal right to adopt since 2005 but remain a small proportion of the total number of adopters. National statistics show that annually around 60 children are adopted by gay couples and a further 60 by lesbian couples.

The Bill that brought about the change was fiercely contested and took three years to pass through Parliament. Issues raised in the debate included concerns that children adopted by same-sex couples would face bullying from peers and worries that children's own gender identity might be skewed by being raised by parents of the same sex.

Responses from the same-sex parents, adopted children themselves and the children's teachers indicates that these issues do not appear to be a significant problem – although the researchers, and some parents themselves, acknowledge that problems of bullying could become a problem as the children become teenagers.

The majority of the children in the study appeared to be adjusting well to family life and to school. Face-to-face interviews with parents, and with those children willing and old enough to take part, showed that parents talked openly with their children about adoption and recognised the value of children maintaining contact with their birth parents.

Some interesting differences emerged in parents' well-being across the three types of family. Gay fathers were significantly less likely to report having depressive symptoms than lesbian mothers and heterosexual couples, most probably reflecting the lower levels of depression shown by men than women generally. However, it should be noted that the level of depression reported by lesbian mothers and heterosexual parents was below, or in line with, the national picture for mental health.

Gay fathers appeared to have more interaction with their children and the children of gay fathers had particularly busy social lives.

Pathways to adoption also differed across the three groups. While most heterosexual couples expected to become parents as a matter of course, fewer same-sex couples expected to have children. This was particularly true of gay fathers, many of whom had viewed their sexual identity as incompatible with parenthood.

Most of the heterosexual couples, and a significant number of lesbian couples, had experienced fertility problems. Many had undergone IVF treatment with no success. In contrast, only one of the gay couples had tried (but failed) to conceive with the help of a surrogate. For the remaining gay couples, adoption was the first choice.

Most parents across the family types had had positive experiences of the adoption process with many speaking warmly of the support they received. A number of same-sex couples, however, reported that agencies lacked experience in working with gay and lesbian parents and that this showed itself in awkwardness. One gay parent described having the phone put down on him when he said that his partner was a man.

Being adopted makes children different to many of their peers: being adopted by same-sex couples could add another dimension to that sense of being different. Interviews with parents showed that they were well aware of the extra challenges they and their children might face – and that they hoped to raise children who were secure in their own identity and valued diversity.

4 March 2013

⇨ The above information is reprinted with kind permission from the University of Cambridge. Please visit www.cam.ac.uk for further information.

The role of the grandparent

By Marilyn Stowe

Earlier in the year, we reported on the case of C (A Child). A grandmother won the right to appeal against a ruling that her grandson be adopted. She had applied for a special guardianship order, an arrangement that would allow her to look after the youngster, providing the stability he needed, without completely torpedoing his relationship to his birth parents.

The Court of Appeal said the original judge had not given sufficient thought to the necessity of adoption and the support which would be available to the mother as if she became the boy's special guardian.

The judge noted the importance of courts only opting for a drastic measure like adoption, permanently removing a child from his or her birth family, when is it really necessary to do so.

It will be interesting to read the eventual outcome of her appeal. But in the meantime, the case highlights the important role grandparents can play in the lives of young children, a role which is perhaps more frequently overlooked now than it once was. Not so long ago, it was routine for parents to turn to their own mothers and fathers living nearby for advice and help with childcare, but nowadays we live in a much more atomised society. Many families are scattered around the country or even the world and the almost invariable result is that grandparents are reduced to the role of occasional visitors rather than the important members of a seamless extended family many once were.

Grandparents who only see their grandchildren occasionally will only have a tenuous relationship with them, of course, one especially prone to the sudden rupturing of divorce or separation. The breakdown of a relationship can have a profound effect on grandparents and they may be left with feelings of grief and loss, even if they never liked their child's spouse.

Not only must they watch as their son's or daughter's life is turned upside down but If they are the paternal grandparents, they must face the very real possibility that they may never see their grandchildren again – unless a strong bond has already been built up between a mother and her former parents-in-law, that is. In other cases, visits may be grudgingly allowed as a kind of trade-off for maintenance payments. If a resident parent is struggling to maintain good relations with their former partner, pressure to maintain regular contact with the former partner's parents may become an additional and unwanted burden.

There are other cases, of course, where the lack of contact results from sheer bloody-mindedness on the part of the resident parent. Having been hurt by the divorce, he or she takes revenge by obstructing the grandparents' access at every possible opportunity, usually with little thought for the children's happiness.

So what legal action is open to grandparents in such situations? In the past, contact orders were occasionally granted to grandparents – but only rarely. Today, however, they have become increasingly common as the courts increasingly recognise the importance of extended family members in the welfare of children.

Anyone can apply to a court for contact with a child, but there would need to be unusual circumstances for a grandparent to make a sole application. The courts will first consider the need for parental contact and may feel that there isn't much time left for the grandparents beyond that. Nothing, of course, prevents extended family members from seeing the children during parental visits.

If you wish to apply for contact with a grandchild, you must first apply to the court for 'leave' to be heard. As the grandparent or step-parent you do not have parental responsibility, so you are not automatically entitled to make a court application in relation to a child. The court will consider the family circumstances and the role played by the grandparent within the family. For example, the court will distinguish between a grandparent who frequently assists with childcare and a grandparent who lives out of the country and sees their grandchild once every few years.

Once leave is obtained, the court will consider the practicalities. It will take into account the children's wishes and feelings, as well as their established routine. Courts will prefer to make provision for the children to see grandparents within existing contact arrangements if possible, rather than carve the children's time into smaller portions. The courts will also consider whether an actual legal order is needed or whether the family can reach an agreement amongst themselves.

They will normally also ask Cafcass to become involved as it is able to interview all parties and speak to the children. Its role in such issues is to investigate, take part in discussions and report to the judge with recommendations.

Sometimes, in more troubled families, grandparents may apply to take over the care of the grandchildren altogether – as in the case we highlighted earlier. But the courts will not give grandparents parental responsibility unless they already have a residence order, specifying that the children should live with them. And without parental responsibility a grandparent does not have the right to any say in schooling or medical treatment for example. But unless the children already live with the grandparents, the courts are unlikely to make that residence order, except in extreme circumstances where one or both of the parents are dead or thought to be incapable of looking after the children.

My advice would certainly be to discuss matters with the child's parents at an early stage. Make it clear that you are not taking sides and that you simply want an on-going role in your grandchild's life. Don't play the blame game or get involved in the specifics of the divorce or separation.

But if that doesn't work or you become worried about your grandchildren, don't let the situation escalate. Instead, seek legal advice.

Finally – be realistic. If the grandchildren are only seeing your son or daughter once a fortnight, it is unlikely that you yourself will see them as much as you may like. Consider whether your application for a contact order should be linked to any issued by your son or daughter. And think too, about your role to date in the lives of your grandchildren. The courts will be more willing to consider an application by a grandparent to assist with childcare if you have historically been the babysitter of choice.

Note: Marilyn Stowe is the Senior Partner at Stowe Family Law LLP, the UK's largest speciality law firm.

20 September 2013

⇨ The above information is reprinted with kind permission from Marilyn Stowe. Please visit www.marilynstowe.co.uk for further information.

© Marilyn Stowe 2013

What rights do grandparents have to their grandchildren?

By Punam Denley

The Government signalled this week in a letter to MPs its intent to introduce legislation, not only to give fathers equal parenting rights, but also to oblige the courts to consider grandparents' rights on the breakdown of a relationship. The high cost of childcare in the UK, as compared with other countries, means that grandparents are increasingly taking over a child-rearing role. Upon a separation or a divorce, the impact of the severance of that close bond between child and grandparent can be felt very keenly. It is a fact that the role of the grandparent is often downplayed and underestimated in the battle that can ensue between the parents.

First steps

Many grandparents are able to continue to see their grandchildren through visits brought about by the children's parent, that is, their son or daughter. This may not always be the case, particularly if the separation is acrimonious. If you find yourself in the situation where you are losing, or have lost, access to your grandchildren, the first step you must do is to attempt to communicate with the child's parent who is causing the problem with contact, if your own child cannot intervene. This can often be difficult but often, an olive branch attempt, to communicate with the mother directly, can lead to resolution in access situations. Grandparents who have a strong bond with their grandchildren and refuse to take sides in the impending separation tend to fare well. A well-written letter to the parent requesting access, yet stating they will not interfere or get involved in any subsequent parental arguments can often open communication levels, leading to a suitable resolution. When seeing the children, the single most important thing is not to denigrate or criticise the parent, as this will almost always be reported back, resulting in disastrous consequences for your relationship with your grandchild.

Mediation

If this attempt does not work, the next step would be mediation through court. You can request mediation, but the other party must also agree to this. Sometimes it is impossible to get agreement on even going to mediation in extreme cases and therefore might not be a suitable step for you to take. Another way could be to arrange a family counselling session, involving the children themselves, especially if they are teenagers. Depending on the maturity of the children, they quite often would like their views aired and taken into account during a breakdown, and it may well be in their interests for that to take place.

Contact order

Only parents can automatically apply for a Contact Order. The law allows for grandparents to apply for leave (permission of the court) to make an application. In simple terms, this means you must apply to be able to be considered for contact. Here, you will be asked to demonstrate to the court, that you have a long-standing and loving bond with the children in question, and that you do not pose a risk to their emotional or physical well-being. If you are granted leave, a report may be made regarding the welfare issues of the child. If such a report is ordered to be prepared, a Children and Family Court Advisory and Support Service (Cafcass) officer will be appointed to assist the court in coming to a decision.

If the report is shown to be favourable to you, this can often persuade the parent with care to come to an agreement. However, if this is not the case, the court will make a decision based on what is in the best interests of the child. Ultimately the judge will rule on whether and what contact will take place, but will be heavily influenced by the views of the Cafcass officer, and will need to give good reasons from departing from the report.

Separations can be difficult and emotions are clearly running high at this particular time. When children are at their most vulnerable during a separation, the role of the grandparent can be crucial in providing the loving care and stability, away from any domestic disputes. Unfortunately, as the law currently stands, grandparents do not have an automatic right to access to their grandchildren. But in my experience, judges recognise the importance of grandparents and do grant contact/access orders, where it is in the children's best interests; unless it really would cause so much disharmony at home that the children would be adversely affected. Normally, such disagreements are dealt with, far away from court, when the dust has been allowed to settle following a marital breakup. If resolution can be sought and maintained through mediation, for the best interests of the children, this would be the practical solution during a painful time.

Note: Punam Denley is the Senior Partner at Blanchards Law.

September 2013

⇨ The above information is reprinted with kind permission from Blanchards Law. Please visit www.blanchardslaw.co.uk/blog for further information.

New study reveals common stumbling blocks for step-families

A third of step-parents have such a difficult relationship with their step-children they cannot wait until they leave home.

A study examining the complicated dynamics facing those who leave an existing partner to 'take on' another's family, found that despite the increasing number of modern families comprising of more than one set of parents, many find it a struggle coping with the trials and tribulations which come with the territory.

As well as adapting to becoming a parent to someone else's child – often soon after a traumatic separation or divorce – step-parents also find themselves at loggerheads with their new partners with issues such as discipline and money (regular stumbling blocks).

Other fall outs included rows over whether they were being 'spoilt' or allowed to 'get away' with too much, the kids playing parents off against each other and ex-partners either demanding too much money or not being willing to fairly contribute towards the costs involved with bringing up the children.

Anastasia de Waal, Chair of Family Lives said: 'When two families merge into one it's always going to be tricky but with the right support and when people focus on being fair and talk through issues and maintain a civil relationship with their partner a lot of these difficulties can and will disappear.'

'Putting the children first and seeking impartial and non-judgemental support, counselling and advice from experts ensures that people are in a better position to develop positive relationships with new additions to their blended family.'

As many as half of the step-parents who took part in the research said they had come close to breaking up with their other half as a result of a bust-up over the children, leading many to admit they are looking forward to them flying the nest as 'it will make life easier'.

The *Family Dynamics* report, carried out among 1,000 step-parents by law firm Slater & Gordon also found two-thirds of those who took part in the research feel they will never be 'fully accepted' by their new family.

Yesterday, Amanda McAlister, family lawyer at Slater & Gordon, said; 'The simple fact is that the traditional family dynamic is a thing of the past, and families come in all shapes and sizes now. So a report like this is really quite sad.

'People need to rise above the difficulties that they have experienced in their marriage and if they get very clear and well documented arrangements for residency and what each person's obligations are then the process can be done amicably.

'Mediation can often be crucial for couples to remain harmonious after a divorce and can often help make sure that the process of separation is considered fair by all parties. If everyone agrees the arrangements are fair it makes the process a lot easier and paves the way for a step-parent to be in the best possible position to build a rewarding and positive relationship with their step-child.'

The research uncovered a string of major flashpoints and trigger topics including many which push parental relationships to the brink of destruction.

These included negotiating holidays and half-term breaks with the child's biological parents, not being included in 'family events' and how to get on with the ex.

More than a quarter of step-parents have to spend time alone at Christmas or Easter while their partner spends time with their ex and the kids.

Additionally, as many as one in four step-parents admit they feel like they are in competition with their step-children's biological parents at Christmas and on their birthdays.

And a similar number claimed they were regularly embroiled in disputes with step-children which resulted in insults such as 'you're not my real parent' being hurled at them.

Other typical barbed comments include: 'I hate you', and 'things were fine before you came along'.

Another bone of contention is their current partner's ex – 15 per cent said they 'don't get on at all with them'.

Amanda McAlister, family lawyer at Slater & Gordon said: 'Residency arrangements are often key here, and the best thing to do is to consult with a legal expert to make sure all the pitfalls and areas that could cause problems and resentment are discussed and covered from the very beginning.

'Relationships are hard but to hear that some step-parents are considering ending a relationship over their partner's children is sad and unnecessary. There are always ways to resolve conflict and come to an amicable agreement.'

Just 17 per cent of those who were polled said they enjoyed a 'positive' relationship with the children's actual parent.

Of the step-parents that have their own biological children, 26 per cent said they couldn't help but compare the behaviour of their own kids against that of their partners.

And 15 per cent said they rarely or never have a pleasant conversation with their step-children.

But that's hardly surprising when more than one in ten said their step-kids regularly screamed at them and blamed them if they didn't get their way.

20 September 2013

⇨ The above information is reprinted with kind permission from Family Lives. Please visit www.familylives.org.uk for further information.

Banning the 'blended' family: why step-families will never be the same as first families

Step-families aren't families in the traditional sense, so let's ban the idealistic language and get realistic about second marriages with children, says Wednesday Martin.

'Natural family'
'Failed marriage'
'Broken family'
'New wife'
'Stepmonster'

Living, researching and writing about step-family life for over a decade, I've witnessed the power of words to shape attitudes and feelings. 'Wicked stepmother' can bring the most loving, self-confident woman with step-kids to her knees. The dated and Dickensian 'broken family', still popular in the British press, perpetuates the inaccurate, damaging view that children and adults can never recover from divorce. 'Co-wives,' a trendy term for ex-wives and 'new wives' who put aside their differences to 'co-parent the kids,' suggests something much creepier – that step-family life is akin to polygamy and that the ladies should be not only united caretakers but also BFFs. Ewww!

With one in three people in the UK now a step-parent, step-child, adult step-child, step-sibling or step-grandparent, can we please resolve to clean up our language in 2013? Top of the hit list: 'blended family'.

'What's wrong with that?' you ask. It has an upbeat and optimistic sound. It's supportive and non-judgemental. Right? Actually, for those who live in step-families, the term and all it implies are like poison.

Why 'blended' is damaging

Ignorance about the reality of step-family life is what sinks the up to 72 per cent of remarriages with children that end in divorce. Consider a typical story:

Hopeful that he is 'fixing' the emotional pain he and his kids have been through, a divorced dad remarries – mostly likely, statistics tell us, before his ex-wife does. Dad and his bride might feel her role is to help heal emotional scars, set the family on course and be 'another mother'.

In this powerful and common fantasy, parent, kids of any age and step-parent don't just get along. They 'blend' into a semblance of a first family, with the step-parent 'loving those kids just like they're my own' and the kids returning the sentiment.

Who can blame them for their high hopes? After all, anyone in a remarriage with kids has likely been bludgeoned with the term and the idea by the media, well-intentioned friends, books on the topic of 'blended family life' and even therapists who specialise in treating 'blended families'.

It's hard to imagine a more harmful concept. Because re-partnership with children or adult children is anything but an ambrosial smoothie. The dad who wants his kids to love his new wife as much as he does quickly realises they don't. The step-mother with good intentions often becomes a target for resentment about all the changes in their lives, and is frequently blamed for their mother's unhappiness, too.

Reaching out to the kids (or their mum) to bridge the gap can backfire, creating feelings of failure and disappointment that in turn stress the couple. Indeed, it may come as a surprise to the general public (and a relief to step-families) to learn that conflict is the rule, rather than the exception, in the first years of step-family life.

These 'family' members are more likely to argue, seethe with jealousy or simply distrust one other than they are to meld into a happy mix right away. It's normal. But thanks to the 'blended' paradigm, they are bound to wonder, 'What are we doing wrong? Why don't we feel like a first family?' 'Why aren't we blended yet?'

Let's break it down

First of all, step-families are not precisely families. They bring together a cast of characters, often under one roof, who aren't related and may have been raised in entirely different ways. Second, step-families often span two households, with kids making potentially stressful trips back and forth. Third, there's an ex or deceased spouse in the picture. And fourth, step-kids, step-parents and parents in step-families face social bias and ignorance – the view that they are second best or abnormal.

Every time we use the term 'blended family' we pretend these important differences between first and step-families, or between first and subsequent marriages, don't exist. We perpetuate the idea that melding should be the goal – and that looking, feeling and acting like a first family is the only measure of success. This straight-jacket of expectations stresses all the players, preventing them from connecting in authentic ways. As one teen girl I interviewed told me of her dad's wife, 'I like her, but I don't want her to be my mum!'

Hope for steps

Step-families succeed, experts tell us, when the couple accepts that there's nothing wrong with a kid preferring her own parent, or a parent feeling closer to his own child. Many step-families can have a dorm-like feel – where she and he both bring their own kids to the mix, step-family members might eat at different times, have two Christmas trees, even elect not to take all their vacations together. When kids are older and living apart, even less bonded-ness is common.

It seems this very flexibility – what might seem like 'lack of closeness' or 'failure to blend' – is critical to step-parents and step-children of any age developing positive relationships in their own way, in their own time. A step-mother may be more like an aunt than a mum to her teenaged step-daughter. A step-father and his busy adult step-son who lives across the country may figure out that cordiality and support, rather than 'close friendship' or 'fatherhood', suit them both. They are resetting their own expectations – and ignoring those who believe they 'ought to be' any particular way.

The National Stepfamily Resource Center has repeatedly called for therapists and the media to stop using the term 'blended family'. It notes that flexibility and respect for difference are better predictors of stepfamily success than 'tight knitted-ness'.

Sure, it makes everyone else feel comfortable when step-families are 'just like' first families. But it doesn't feel so great to step-families themselves. So please, don't call us 'blended'.

Dr Wednesday Martin, a social anthropologist and writer, is the author of Stepmonster: A New Look at Why Real Stepmothers Think, Feel and Act the Way We Do. *Her new book,* Primates of Park Avenue, *is due to be published in 2014.*

23 January 2013

⇨ The above information is reprinted with kind permission from *The Telegraph*. Please visit www.telegraph.co.uk for further information.

© Dr Wednesday Martin/ The Telegraph 2013

Top ten tips for a happier family

1. Balancing work and home life

It's not easy balancing your work and home life, but how you manage it can make quite a difference to your relationship with your family. Having a balance between work and home – being able to work in a way which fits around family commitments and isn't restricted to the nine to five – boosts self-esteem as you're not always worrying about neglecting your responsibilities in any area, making you feel more in control of your life. Your family will be happier to see more of you, and you'll have a life away from home.

2. Look after yourself

Parents often spend all their time looking after everyone else in the family and forget about themselves. If you don't look after yourself, you can end up feeling miserable and resentful, and you won't be able to give your children the support they need. Admit to yourself that you actually have feelings and needs of your own. It's not selfish to treat yourself once in a while! It doesn't have to be expensive – but putting aside some time to do just what YOU want to do, even if it's only ten minutes a day – is so important.

3. Discipline

Rather than thinking of discipline as a punishment, you should use it as a way of teaching your children how to meet their needs without hurting or offending anyone. While you may be angry, it can help to keep calm and teach your child how he or she could have handled the situation differently, and how he or she can go about it differently next time. This way is both more positive and more constructive.

4. Setting boundaries

We often use boundaries to protect children from harm or danger. But it is important that you try to explain why boundaries are there, rather than issuing orders – for instance, if you pull them away from an open fire explain why. Children may be reluctant to follow instructions if parents command them. However, an explanation as to why the instructions are important will help your child understand, and therefore cooperate.

5. Communication

Communication is important – during both the good and the tough times. Children often find it hard to put their feelings into words and just knowing that their parents are listening can be enough. Talk about yourself – not just about your problems but about your daily life. If they feel included in the things you do they are more likely to see the value of including you in the things they do.

6. Quality time

Try to organise some time together as a family a few times a week – perhaps three meals a week you could sit down to eat as a family. This will give you all a chance to connect and talk about the important issues, as well as the more fun topics. Ask your children to help you with the chores or to run errands. They may protest but they will feel included in your life rather than being an outsider.

7. Joint decisions

With older children, it is normal for them to test the limits of boundaries to see what they can get away with. You may need to adapt boundaries as children grow into teens – it can even help to involve your child in the negotiation of new boundaries. Too many restrictions will be hard to keep on top of, so it is a good idea to work out which boundaries are really important to you, such as the ones for your children's safety, and which boundaries are not worth fighting about. With fewer restrictions, your children will appreciate that the boundaries you do set are serious.

8. Comforting

It is important for a family to be there for each other through the hard times, as well as the good times. If there is a family tragedy, or a family member has a problem, pulling together can really help. Your children will need your help at this time, and it is important to be open and communicate with them. They will need reassurance and explanation, and will react differently depending on their ages. It can also help to talk to someone impartial.

9. Be flexible

More than anything, children just want to spend time with their parents. It can be lots of fun to make time for an impromptu game or an unscheduled trip to the park, as well as being something that you and your children will remember fondly. It's good to have a routine, but it's not the end of the world if it's interrupted from time to time for spontaneous fun and games. For busy families, it can be useful to schedule in a few hours every now and then for a lazy afternoon together.

10. Spend quality time with your partner

It can be difficult to find time for you and your partner once you have children, but it is important to make time for each other. After all, children learn about relationships from their parents. Make sure you communicate with them frequently about all the day-to-day matters, as well as just things you enjoy talking about. Try to organise time that you can spend with each other, whether it's going out for a meal, or just relaxing in front of the TV together.

⇨ The above information is reprinted with kind permission from Family Lives. Please visit www.familylives.org.uk for further information.

© Family Lives 2013

Family incomes and savings rise but household debt levels reach an all time high

⇨ Average debts peak at almost £13,000 – highest recorded by report series.

⇨ But family incomes increase by more than £1,200 a year.

⇨ More families get into a regular savings habit, reaching a record high of £96 a month.

UK families are experiencing a mixed bag of financial fortunes, the latest *Aviva Family Finances Report* reveals today. The report, which tracks the financial circumstances of different UK family types, shows that while incomes and savings habits are sneaking upwards, so are typical debts.

Typical family debts stack up to record levels

Despite their growing incomes and a greater commitment to saving every month, UK families are regularly turning to unsecured borrowing. Typical household debt has increased by 38% since May 2012 (£9,314) and now stands at £12,834, the highest since this report series began in January 2011.

The biggest debts have actually been racked up through loans from friends and family, at an average of £2,011 per household, while credit cards add a further £2,006 and personal loans an additional £1,959. Five per cent of families say they now rely on payday loans and a further 3% make use of pawnbrokers.

It is therefore a slight concern that the percentage of families making monthly debt repayments has fallen consistently in the last 12 months from 57% in August 2012 to 51% in January 2013 and just 45% in July 2013.

Good news as family income increases slightly

More positively however, UK families' typical monthly net income in July 2013 fell just short of the highest figure ever recorded by the report series, which was £2,150 in April 2012.

With £2,108 at their disposal each month – 5% more than a year ago – the typical family has £1,260 more spending power over 12 months than they did in August 2012 when the typical monthly income was £2,003.

Regular family savings see a surge

This extra income appears to be having a beneficial impact on people's monthly saving habits. The typical family saves or invests £96 per month in July 2013, up by 20% from £80 in January to set a new record for the *Family Finances Report*.

For the first time since the series began, fewer than one in three families save nothing each month (31%) – a significant improvement on the 40% recorded in January 2011. This edition also breaks new ground in terms of the number of families with no savings put away: down to 23% from a high of 33% in January 2011.

Expenses fall as families cut back on holidays and luxuries

The improvement in savings habits marries up with the fact that typical monthly expenditure among UK families fell for the first time since November 2011. The July 2013 average of £1,748 represents a fall of 4% from the peak of £1,819 in January 2013.

Luxury items are among the first to go when it comes to trimming household expenses. While spending on food has gone up by £14 a month across all families in the last six months alone – equivalent to £168 per year – a range of non-essential items including satellite TV subscriptions and recreation have all been scaled back to compensate. Financial constraints also appear to be prompting more families to forego a holiday this year, with 51% spending on this expense in July 2013 compared with 54% in August 2012.

Louise Colley, protection distribution director for Aviva says: 'Since we began our report series, we've seen a common thread of people juggling their finances to balance the family books. As money matters improve in one area, this is often offset in another – and this edition is no different. It's great to see that families are saving more than ever, but slightly concerning that debt levels are continuing to climb.

'Building a savings pot is a fantastic step, but if debts are growing, families need to consider which is the more pressing need. We'd also urge people to take further steps and think about family protection to cover them against a sudden loss of income. Notably 55% of families say that unexpected expenses are one of their biggest financial fears so having this cover in place can provide invaluable peace of mind.'

Methodology

Data was sourced from the *Aviva Family Finances Report* series which used findings from over 18,000 people who are members of one of the six groups of families identified above via Canadean research. This report is a definitive look at the personal finances of families in the UK. Not only does it look at personal wealth, income sources and expenditure patterns but also tracks how these change across the different types of family unit.

In addition to the regular data, in each edition a spotlight will be shone onto a different relevant topic. This issue has a focus on how the cost of sending children to school impacts on family finances.

10 July 2013

⇨ The above information is reprinted with kind permission from Aviva. Please visit www.aviva.co.uk for further information.

© Aviva 2013

Families with children will be most affected by falling incomes, study finds

⇨ Grim predictions for UK family finances up to 2015 revealed in new evidence produced by the Institute for Fiscal Studies (IFS) for the Family and Childcare Trust.

⇨ The median income among families with children is projected to fall between 2010 and 2015 by 4.2 per cent. For a couple with two children this equates to £1,250 less a year by 2015.

⇨ Families with children aged under five, families with more than two children and lone parent families not in paid work bear the biggest financial pain in years ahead.

An IFS report, commissioned by the Family and Childcare Trust, is the first to reveal the prospects for poverty rates and income for different family types up to the year 2015.

The study has found

The median (middle) household with children faces an average drop in income of 4.2 per cent by 2015–16, equivalent to an annual income drop of £1,250 for a couple with two children. The 4.2 per cent average drop for families with children is significantly higher than the loss for the median household overall, which is 0.9 per cent. This is equivalent to a reduction in annual income of £215 for a couple without children.

Families with children under five will experience a significant financial hit. Between 2010–11 and 2015–16, 500,000 more children will fall into absolute poverty as defined by the Child Poverty Act (2010), where the poverty line is fixed at 60 per cent of the median income in 2010–11. 300,000 of these children come from households where the youngest child is under five. The median household with a child under five faces a drop in income of 4.9 per cent by 2015–16.

Larger families will suffer a disproportionate financial hit. For example, the median household with three children will see their income fall by 6.8 per cent by 2015–16, compared to the median household with one child which will see it fall by 3.3 per cent.

These patterns have a differential impact on children from ethnic minority groups who tend to have more children per family. For example, the absolute and relative poverty rates for Pakistani and Bangladeshi children increases by more than five percentage points by 2015–16 (the relative increase is from 49.2 per cent to 54.6 per cent and the absolute increase is from 49.2 per cent to 55.8 per cent).

Tax and benefit changes

The study also examines the impact of tax and benefit changes to be introduced between 2010–11 and 2014–15 on different family types. It confirms that families with children will lose more through tax and benefit changes than pensioners or adults without children – before and after the introduction of Universal Credit. This reflects the fact that benefits for those of working age are being cut, and families with children are more reliant on benefits than those without children.

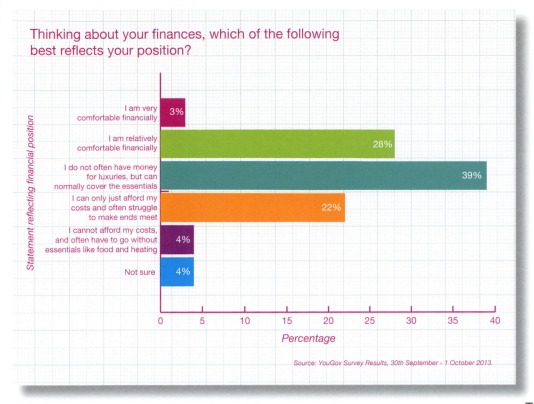

Thinking about your finances, which of the following best reflects your position?

Statement reflecting financial position:
- I am very comfortable financially — 3%
- I am relatively comfortable financially — 28%
- I do not often have money for luxuries, but can normally cover the essentials — 39%
- I can only just afford my costs and often struggle to make ends meet — 22%
- I cannot afford my costs, and often have to go without essentials like food and heating — 4%
- Not sure — 4%

Percentage (x-axis: 0, 5, 10, 15, 20, 25, 30, 35, 40)

Source: YouGov Survey Results, 30th September - 1 October 2013.

The UK's poorest families with children lose the largest proportion of their income from tax and benefit changes. Before taking Universal Credit into account, families in the poorest income decile will be ten per cent worse off in 2014–15 than they would have been had no changes been made to the tax and benefit system. Even after the introduction of Universal Credit, this group loses more than average, at just over six per cent. In particular, lone parents not in employment lose more than 12 per cent of their income on average as a result of tax and benefit changes to be introduced between 2010–11 and 2014–15, or £2,000 per year.

The Government's plan to introduce Universal Credit will soften the blow for certain family types but will not be introduced fully in place for existing claimants until 2018. The report offers evidence that although Universal Credit strengthens work incentives for most individuals, it weakens the incentive for a second earner in a couple, typically the mother in a couple household, to take up employment.

'Lone parents not in employment lose more than 12 per cent of their income on average as a result of tax and benefit changes'

Carers will suffer a disproportionate financial hit. Average loss from tax and benefit changes for households claiming carer's allowance is just over six per cent, compared to a loss of just over four per cent (pre or post-Universal Credit) for all households.

A spokesperson for the Family and Childcare Trust said: 'These figures reveal the full extent to which families with children are shouldering the burden of austerity. Having children has always been expensive. But now many families with children face an extra penalty of more than £1,000.'

'It is particularly surprising to see that some of the most vulnerable groups – such as families with new babies and lone parents out of work – are bearing the brunt of the tax and benefit reforms. Many families will be left struggling to understand why they have been singled out in this way and how this sits alongside the Government's ambition for the UK to become a family friendly nation.'

The full report, entitled *The Impact of Austerity Measures on Households with Children* can be found at www.familyandchildcaretrust.org.

The Family and Childcare Trust released the report as part of its national Family Friendly scheme, which aims to make the UK more supportive of family life. See www.wearefamilyfriendly.org for more details.

Newsdesk notes

Before or after the introduction of Universal Credit, families with children will lose part of their income through tax and benefit changes:

⇨ Households with children lose six per cent on average

⇨ All households lose four per cent

⇨ Working-age households without children lose three per cent on average

⇨ Pensioner households lose less than two per cent on average

⇨ The overall average loss is four per cent.

The report urges caution over the statistics on Pakistani and Bangladeshi families, due to the small sample size for this group.

4 January 2012

⇨ The above information is reprinted with kind permission from the Family and Childcare Trust. Please visit www.familyandchildcaretrust.org for further information.

© 2013 Family and Childcare Trust

Relationship charity reveals one in three new parents feel stressed about money

New research published Tuesday 25 June by the relationship charity OnePlusOne shows that money worries are the main cause of stress for one-third of new parents (33%).

The new report, *Can we afford a baby and not break up?* shows that many new parents are not prepared for the financial impact of a new baby and how this will affect their relationship. The Money Advice Service estimates the cost of a new baby at between £1,600 and £7,200, in their first year.

Director of OnePlusOne Penny Mansfield said:

'There is little that can compare with the excitement of having a new baby, but it can put severe financial strain on new parents, especially now, when prices are rising and pay is falling. Existing debt, new expenses and losing one income is a triple whammy for new parents that can easily lead to arguments about money and cause relationships to break down. With the cost of family breakdown standing at £46 billion per year investing in family services is definitely cost effective.'

The transition to parenthood is a particularly difficult time for couples, as a new baby puts them under pressures they may never have experienced before. Reducing to a single income, as one partner stops work, can change the nature of the relationship to the more traditional roles of homemaker and breadwinner.

Julia McGinley, Head of Support at Netmums.com said:

'Money can't buy the happiness a new baby brings, but there is no way round the fact that new babies do cost a lot of money. New mums often say that they feel uncomfortable having to ask for money instead of having their own income as it's not something most women are used to doing. Almost half of mums feel stressed about the dilemma of whether to work or not, and those that eventually stay home worry about the loss of income. But knowing there is help available to work through your situation and help set a manageable budget will be a big comfort to new mums.'

Penny Mansfield continued:

'When planning for a baby, new parents need to consider the financial impact and how to manage sensitive discussions about money and their new roles without falling out. To keep their relationship strong, couples should plan ahead, agree a budget and keep talking – it's important that they share their feelings and support one another.'

Chief Executive of Family Matters Institute who run www.DAD.info, Matt Buttery said:

'The good news is that help is at hand to keep relationships strong. New dads and mums can find practical advice to pull their finances into shape and even talk to other parents about their relationship online. We've found it's possible to cut tens, sometimes hundreds of pounds a month off household spending without missing out on any of the essentials that you and your family need, and for many that online support they've found from others has been life changing.'

Notes to editors

⇨ OnePlusOne is a UK charity, which aims to strengthen relationships; helping couples and parents through a range of online resources including the Couple Connection and the Parent Connection. It provides online training for frontline family workers to equip them with the skills to offer timely relationship support in a face-to-face setting. Based on latest research evidence, it promotes early action to equip couples to deal with relationship issues before they become entrenched.

⇨ ICM surveyed 1,403 parents, including 512 new parents who have one child under the age of three. The research was carried out between 19 and 24 April 2003. ICM also hosted an online community and followed focus groups to gather qualitative data referred to in the report.

⇨ OnePlusOne was recently commissioned by the Department for Education to lead a high-profile campaign to encourage couples to see seeking support as normal in strengthening their relationship. The charity will be working with expert partners, including Working Families, Contact a Family, DAD.info, Netmums, Student Room and YouthNet, to create online spaces where couples can find tools to help themselves.

⇨ The Relationships Foundation, a think-tank on relationships and society, calculated the cost of family breakdown as £46 billion in March 2013. For more information visit their website www.relationshipsfoundation. org.

25 June 2013

⇨ The above information is reprinted with kind permission from OnePlusOne. For more information, visit the websites www.oneplusone.org.uk,www. dad.info or www.netmums. com.

Parents give up work as childcare costs outstrip income

⇨ Financially unprotected families left vulnerable as they rely on one salary.

⇨ 32,000 more women choose to stay at home to take care of their families.

⇨ School inflation hits 6.89% as parents pay £111 per month on school extras.

Parents are questioning whether they can both afford to work, due to the high cost of childcare. According to new research from Aviva, a working mother could be up to £98 a month worse off after all child and work costs are taken into account.

As a result, thousands of families could be left in the potentially vulnerable position of relying on a single salary. More worrying still, the Aviva study shows 95% of UK families don't feel completely financially protected against the loss of an income.

The findings are highlighted in Aviva's latest *Family Finances Report* which is released today. This edition shines a spotlight on the challenges faced by working parents, and the fact that the majority of these families are worryingly under-protected financially.

Significant childcare costs

An in-depth analysis of childcare costs reveals the financial struggles that many working parents face, with typical full-time care costing £385 per month per child. Parents who need full-time care for children under two have to pay the most (£729 per month) while those with older children who need part-time care pay the least (£78 per month).

While 54% of families claim they don't use childcare and 31% say their family/friends provide this for free, those parents who do pay can find it incredibly difficult to juggle their finances. Even those who don't pay for childcare find that they are spending an average of £111 per month on child-related expenses such as sports activities, food at school, clothing and transport – costs which have seen inflation of 6.89% over the last year.

Cost of employment

In addition to childcare and schooling costs, the average working family member spends £120 per month (full-time) and £90 per month (part-time) on expenses associated with employment such as transport, food and clothing.

Therefore – when all costs are taken into account – the average woman with two children (one-year- and seven-years-old) would be out of pocket by £98 per month if she worked part time, and better off by just £120 per month if she worked full time. While Government benefits could provide some support, many families have seen cuts in this area and may need to consider whether this kind of support is sustainable going forward.

Single income families leave themselves exposed

With some women finding their income eroded by the associated costs of working, it is unsurprising that 32,000 more women have chosen to stay at home to look after their families since the third quarter of 2010. However, while this can make financial sense, it can leave families in a vulnerable position if the main breadwinner is unable to work for any reason.

Worryingly few families appear to be taking proactive steps to protect themselves: 60% are without life insurance, 85% are without critical illness cover and 90% are without income protection. Instead, should the average family lose one income, they would look to cut spending to a minimum (51%), turn to the Government for help (28%) or dip into their savings (25%). Although with average savings at just £982, or under half a month's income, this is unlikely to last long.

If they were faced with a permanent loss of an income, families' immediate worries would be about meeting their bills (71%), maintaining their standard of living (42%) and being forced to move home (37%) – all stressful issues to deal with at a time of great need.

Children are also a major concern in this scenario, with 29% of parents worried about how this might impact on their behaviour and 23% concerned about their performance at school.

Louise Colley, head of protection for Aviva and mum to four-year-old twins comments: 'This report shows very clearly the challenge many families with young children face as they balance their income with the cost of childcare. As care costs rise, it's quite possible we will see more and more couples relying on one salary while the other person looks after the children – simply because they may actually be worse off if both people work.

However, while this may make financial sense, it can also leave families vulnerable should anything happen to that income earner.

'Families today face an array of money worries, as this report shows. But the unintended consequences of not having protection in place can be huge – both financially and emotionally – should the unexpected happen. 60% of families don't have even basic life insurance so we'd strongly urge all families to consider the 'what ifs' and take steps to make sure they're covered. After all, we go out to work to do the best for our families but if we don't have suitable protection, we could be leaving them financially exposed.'

31 August 2011

⇨ The above information is reprinted with kind permission from Aviva. Please visit www.aviva.co.uk for further information.

Child maintenance is crucial for single parents in the UK

by Janet Allbeson, Senior Policy Adviser at Gingerbread

If you're a single parent in the UK, you're more likely to be struggling – more single parents than couple families have no savings, or are in social housing. But child maintenance – the money single parents receive from the child's other parent – has the potential to really make a difference. Janet Allbeson, Senior Policy Adviser at Gingerbread, explains why the Government shouldn't start charging for their Child Support Agency services, which help many single parents get the child maintenance arrangement they need.

The majority of the British public think the Government should set – and enforce – how much in child maintenance payments single parents should receive from their child's other parent. So why isn't this message getting through to the Government?

Child maintenance can make a huge, practical difference for single parent families. It can help pay fuel bills, buy clothes for children or fund school trips that are otherwise a real stretch. For particularly financially vulnerable

families, including single parent families on benefits, it can also be the difference between children growing up in poverty and not.

When it's paid, child maintenance pulls one in five single parent families on benefit out of poverty – but almost two-thirds of these families aren't receiving it.

At a time when benefits are falling and prices rising, a report released earlier this month from Gingerbread, *Kids Aren't Free*, shows just how important child maintenance is for struggling parents on benefit raising their children alone.

A vital resource for single parent families

Since 2010, single parents receiving out-of-work benefits have been able to keep the full value of any child maintenance they receive, in addition to their benefit payments. This money is crucial: for some households, the money received in child maintenance can make up 12 per cent of their total household income. As one single mother explains: 'It would take me from the breadline to just, sort of, comfortable. It would just mean I could take her out on a whim without thinking "can I afford it?"'

Even though all parents have a responsibility to provide financially for their child, unfortunately paying child maintenance is far too often the exception, rather than the norm. Our research – based on a study of 760 single parents on benefits – showed that only around a third (36 per cent) of single parents on benefit are actually receiving any child maintenance. 'It's

OK when I'm getting paid [for work]', says one single parent we spoke to. 'But then it's irritating when I don't get paid. He should be the one paying it, ensuring his daughter has got enough food and stuff', she explains.

Private arrangements don't always work

For single parents on benefit almost twice as many (37 per cent) rely on the Child Support Agency (CSA) for their child maintenance arrangements compared to those who make their own arrangements with their child's other parent (20 per cent), while 43% have no arrangement at all.

Our research shows that while private arrangements do mostly work well for the one in five on benefits who have them, the economic and relationship circumstances of parents and the length of time since separation, have a large part to play in determining the type of maintenance arrangement they can have. And sometimes single parents struggle to get an arrangement at all, so the CSA really is a crucial service. 'He took all the money out of the bank... and just upped and left', recounts one single mother. 'He wasn't happy setting an agreement up. So I went to them [the CSA], as a last resort'.

Nonetheless, the Government is planning to levy charges for both parents to access the new statutory service that will replace the CSA in the near future, to try to get more parents to make their own arrangements. However, we remain to be convinced that this new system of charging, combined with a number of newly funded 'relationship support' services for separated parents, will lead to more parents collaborating and more poor children getting child maintenance. Instead, we're concerned that parents who are unable to make their own arrangements may be discouraged by the charges from using the statutory service at all.

The impact on child poverty

With 67 per cent of single parents on benefits in the study saying that they wouldn't find it easy to scrape together the £20 upfront fee to use the new statutory service, the risk is that a greater number of poor parents – who would otherwise have turned to the state for necessary help in getting the other parent to pay – will give up altogether on child maintenance.

While child poverty is predicted to rise steeply over the next decade, we know that child maintenance could play a huge role in mitigating that rise. But our research also raises serious questions about the Government's planned approach in helping to achieve this. We hope that our research, as well as the new findings highlighting strong public support for the Government to play a role in setting and enforcing child maintenance payments, give the Government pause for thought as they finalise their plans for the new statutory service. Ultimately, it must do whatever will result in more children getting child maintenance and being lifted out of poverty as a result.

The research for *Kids Aren't Free* was carried out in partnership by Gingerbread, NatCen and Bryson Purdon Social Research, and funded by the Nuffield Foundation.

1 July 2013

⇨ The material on pages 30 and 31, from *Child maintenance is crucial for single parents in the UK* http://www.oxfam.org.uk/uk-poverty-blog/blog/2013/07/child-maintenance-is-crucial-for-single-parents-in-the-uk by Janet Allbeson (Senior Policy Adviser at Gingerbread) is reproduced with the permission of Oxfam GB, Oxfam House, John Smith Drive, Cowley, Oxford OX4 2JY, UK www.oxfam.org.uk. Oxfam GB does not necessarily endorse any text or activities that accompany the materials.

Childcare – where's the emergency?

By Caroline Davey

We had a fire alarm in the Gingerbread offices this week – and the well-practised drill had us all outside within minutes before we got the all-clear to go back inside. There is a nursery in our building, and as we shivered in the cold, we all watched with admiration as the childcare workers got the young children out of the building at lightning speed, all accounted for and kept warm and calm.

It's at times like that you realise just how important those child-to-carer ratios are – and what an impact the Government's latest proposals to increase them could have. Certainly all the childcare staff I saw during the drill looked like they had their hands pretty full taking care of the little ones in their charge under the current ratios, and it was hard to see how they'd have been able to evacuate safely if they had more children to look after – tucked under their arms perhaps?!

It reminded me, yet again, that it's time to sound the alarm on childcare.

The cost and shortage of childcare is harming our economy and our society. Parents who were once an active part of the workforce are giving up their jobs, childcare costs are overtaking mortgage payments and women are being held back from senior positions in all industries.

The evidence is so clear, and the arguments so well-rehearsed, that tackling the childcare problem is absolutely fundamental to addressing a whole host of issues, not least improving maternal employment rates, particularly for single parents. But then why is there still no sense of urgency from the Government to act? And when I say act I don't just mean tinkering round the edges with ratio proposals, but properly biting the bullet and putting serious investment into childcare to fix it once and for all?

Much as we have heard many warm words from the Government about how they understand the importance of childcare, and we even – allegedly – got close to an announcement on investment a few months ago, in the echoing silence since all we actually have are delayed announcements and reports of coalition squabbles over how to spend (any) money.

Which, in itself, shows that they haven't really got it at all. Because if the Government truly acknowledged the crisis that childcare in the UK is in, it would not bicker over which group of female voters to buy off with a small cash injection, it would instead begin a fundamental system reform that would not only help to transform how we work and how we care for our children, but would also significantly strengthen the economy. Just look at all those Scandinavian countries that have childcare sewn up and seem to be weathering the 'global' recession far better than we are.

If declaring a state of emergency is the only way to get politicians to tackle our country's childcare seriously, then it's time to sound the klaxon.

27 February 2013

⇨ The above information is reprinted with kind permission from Caroline Davey, Director of Policy at Gingerbread, the national charity for single parents. Please visit www.gingerbread.org.uk for further information.

Being a teenage parent

By Petra Acred

The statistics

Teenage pregnancy is a social issue that often hits the headlines but, despite growing concern, conception rates in the UK have been steadily declining over the past few years. The under-18 conception rate in the UK for 2010 was the lowest since comparable records began in 1969 at 35.5 conceptions per 1,000 women aged 15- to 17-years-old. In 2010, there was also a 6.8% decline in the number of conceptions to girls under 16 from 2009, and the under-20s was the only age group where conception rates had not increased.

The recent drop in teenage pregnancies has been attributed to:

⇨ improved access to contraceptives and contraceptive publicity

⇨ improved education on sex and relationships

⇨ an increase in young women aspiring towards continuing their education

⇨ an increase in media awareness of young people

⇨ the perception of a stigma attached to being a teenage mother.

Despite this reduction in teenage pregnancies, however, the UK continues to have the highest rate of teenage births and abortions in Western Europe.

The challenges of being a teenage parent

Being a parent comes with enormous responsibility and sacrifice, and facing these new challenges whilst still a teenager can be particularly difficult.

Money matters

Although the most important thing a child can be given is care and attention, they cannot survive on love alone. Supporting a baby can be incredibly expensive, particularly as young parents are more likely to have a lower income. As a baby requires round-the-clock care, there is also less opportunity for the primary care giver (mother or father) to earn extra money by working.

Education

Having a baby while still at school or college can put education and career prospects on hold. It may be very difficult to attend classes, study for exams or keep on top of coursework when there is a baby who needs caring for. The Government's *Care to Learn* scheme, however, covers childcare costs for teenage parents above compulsory school age who want to continue their learning.

So-long social life?

It is often hard for teen-parents to balance their old life with the new challenges of parenthood. Keeping up with friends may be difficult and some young parents feel that they have to grow up very quickly and miss out on the fun of being a teenager.

Stigma

Social stigma surrounding teenage pregnancy has been around for centuries. Life was often made very difficult for girls who found themselves pregnant outside of

marriage and although attitudes have changed, the stigma surrounding teenage pregnancy often remains and can be difficult to cope with.

Unfortunately, assumptions are often made about the quality of a parent based on their age and some teenage parents are bullied and mocked by their peers and others. Stigma is potentially very dangerous, with sex going undiscussed and teenagers feeling as though they have no one to turn to for advice and support.

Support

Finding out that you are about to become a teen-parent can be a scary experience but there are places that you can turn to for advice.

⇨ Sexwise – if you think you might be pregnant and need some confidential advice, you can call the helpline on 0800 282 930.

⇨ Brook – offers free and confidential advice and contraception to those under 25. You can call the helpline on 0808 802 1234 or visit one of their centres around the country. www.brook.org.uk.

⇨ The Young Woman's Guide to Pregnancy – this free guide from the baby charity, Tommy's, can be found at www.tommys.org.

Useful websites

⇨ www.bubbalicious.co.uk – an online support network for young parents.

⇨ www.bestbeginnings.org.uk – a charity that works to give every baby in the UK the healthiest start to life. Lots of useful resources and information.

6 September 2013

⇨ The above information is reprinted with kind permission from the author.

Teenage pregnancy could be 'contagious'

Teenage pregnancy could be 'contagious' for girls influenced by their elder sisters who have children while young, new research has suggested.

A team studied the records of thousands of women and their families over decades and found that those with elder sisters who had children in their teenage years were twice as likely to do the same as those without.

'Previous research has shown that family background and raising the education of girls decreases the chances of teenage pregnancy'

The research by British and Norwegian scientists showed that although there is evidence that better education of women leads to lower teenage pregnancy rates, in families with teenage mothers the chances of a younger girl having a child in her teens doubled from one in five to two in five.

The University of Bristol's Professor Carol Propper, who co-authored the study, said: 'Previous research has shown that family background and raising the education of girls decreases the chances of teenage pregnancy.

'However, these findings reveal the positive sibling effect (on conception rates) still dwarfs the negative effect of education. These findings provide strong evidence that the contagious effect of teen motherhood in siblings is larger than the general effect of being better educated.

'This suggests that more policies aimed directly at decreasing teenage pregnancy may be needed in order to reduce teen births.'

The study – *Is Teenage Motherhood Contagious? Evidence from a Natural Experiment* – saw Prof.

Propper work with scientists from the University of Bergen and the Norwegian School of Economics. They analysed census data from 42,606 Norwegian women who were born after the Second World War and their families as they got older.

They chose to look at sister-to-sister relationships because sisters generally spend more time together than with schoolmates or other friends and are therefore likely to be influenced by the behaviour of their siblings. There is also scientific evidence that suggests younger children in families are influenced by the sexual activity of their older brothers and sisters.

They found that the sibling effect is larger for women from poorer backgrounds but gets smaller as the age gap between sisters increases.

'Those with elder sisters who had children in their teenage years were twice as likely to do the same as those without'

Figures released by the Office for National Statistics in February showed that in 2009, the most recent year for which there are records, the rate of conception among UK women aged 18 and under decreased by 5.9%, from 40.7 conceptions per 1,000 women aged 15 – 17 in 2008 to 38.3 in 2009. Conception rates for women aged under 20 decreased by 4%.

9 August 2011

⇨ The above information is reprinted with kind permission from the Press Association. Please visit www.pressassociation.com for further information.

More support needed for teen dads, charities warn

We need to stop treating fathers like optional extras and help teen dads play a bigger part in their children's lives, leading family charities have said today.

Are we nearly there yet, Dad? (1), a report by the Family Strategic Partnership (2), warns that a culture shift is needed in 'mother-centred' family services which often treat dads as invisible. Currently services across the board, from pregnancy care to housing support, are driving fathers apart from their children through a 'culture where fathers are not valued'.

'We need to... help teen dads play a bigger part in their children's lives'

Issues include:

⇨ a failure by maternity services and children's centres to even ask about fathers (3),

⇨ local authority housing benefit rules that prevent dads from accommodating their children (4),

⇨ a widespread lack of basic local authority data on the numbers and profile of teen fathers (5).

The report, which has been funded by the Department for Education, calls for an 'attitudinal shift' in statutory services such as prisons, schools and health services, towards a culture of support for young dads.

The report recommends that local authorities appoint teen-dad lead professionals to co-ordinate a dad-friendly approach throughout services.

Jonathan Rallings, Barnardo's Assistant Director of Policy and Research, comments:

'For too long dads have been treated either as optional extras or completely invisible by mother-centred family services.

Young dads want to play their part in bringing up their children. However, they all too often receive the message that they're worthless from services that ignore or marginalise them from the point of pregnancy onwards.

To be properly involved in their children's lives, young dads need the same kind of support as teen mums. This includes easily accessible parenting advice, help with housing and special timetabling for training and study.

We are calling on local authorities to help lead a cultural shift in family care, by introducing practices across their services that universally support young dads' journeys into fatherhood.'

Report recommendations include:

⇨ Every local authority should appoint a lead professional for young fathers.

⇨ A systematic approach to data collection on fathers should be developed by central government.

⇨ Relationship support should also help young parents maintain contact and value the father child relationship.

Notes to Editors

(1) *Are we nearly there yet, Dad?*: Supporting young dads' journeys through fatherhood', Barnardo's and Family Strategic Partnership 2012.

(2) The Family Strategic Partnership (FSP) is a consortium of four organisations (Barnardo's, Action for Prisoners' Families, Children England and The Family and Parenting Institute) that have come together to share their vision and experience in the family voluntary, community and social enterprise sector (VCSES). The FSP is led by Barnardo's and works in partnership with the Department for Education (DfE) and the VCSES across England.

(3) Maternity services may systematically exclude young men due to lack of staff awareness and resources. A review of US and UK research studies found young fathers often have limited or no contact with midwives, health visitors and social workers. In many cases, Children's Centres will only ever come into contact with the mother and child.

(4) When young fathers have their children living with them on a part-time basis, decisions can become complicated, and the child's best interests are not necessarily considered. Furthermore, under Local Housing Allowance rules, single people aged under 35 who either do not have children or are not primary carers are normally assumed to be living in shared accommodation.

(5) Data on the number of young fathers in each local authority is not collected.

17 December 2012

⇨ The above information is reprinted with kind permission from Barnardo's, 2013. Please visit www.barnardos.org.uk for further information.

Teenage mums: the real story

Prymface, the 33-year-old mother of a 16-year-old boy, tells the story of her life thus far, describes what it is really like to be a teenage mother and explains why young mothers deserve respect.

I'm pregnant

I got pregnant at 16. Don't judge me; it wasn't deliberate, well not on my part anyway. I remember sitting in McDonalds just after having the test, clutching the selection of pro-life leaflets I'd been given, with my 31-year-old boyfriend (I still believed he was 24 at this point!), feeling kinda numb.

It didn't feel like it was happening to me at all. Maybe if anyone could have seen the situation I was in they would have snatched those pro-life leaflets out of my hands. Even the pro-lifers didn't look too sure that they were doing the right thing. Maybe they remembered my boyfriend from the last time he was there with a scared pregnant 16-year-old.

I went in to college and told my tutor that I'd have to leave, before bursting into tears. She told me that every child was a gift from God. I didn't know if I believed in God but I admired her positivity. I cried some more and agreed to stay on at college, much to my boyfriend's disapproval.

I didn't want to tell anyone else at college about my situation, but I kept nearly passing out on the bus and it started pissing me off that no one would give me a seat. I was so scared about people's reactions that I think I may have outed someone in my effort to dilute the shock of my news. 'Guess what? He's gay and I'm pregnant' seemed to at least divert some of the attention away from me, though I probably ruined the other guy's life.

Once news was out, I quickly had to re-evaluate who I was. I figured the cute, innocent, flirty thing wouldn't really wash anymore, not with the looming bump. When my photography teacher asked what I was doing over summer and I said 'having a baby', she just laughed nervously. My maths teacher would whisper to me that if I didn't do the homework it was OK because he 'knew'.

Friends would dare to reach out and touch my stomach then squeal with a kind of repulsion. I didn't understand this ritual. There didn't seem to be any enjoyment from either party. I tried to keep my fat, ugly bump hidden and I refused to waddle.

I put off telling my parents for as long as possible. I kept telling myself it was only two words. My boyfriend wanted me to say: 'I'm having a baby.' He said it sounded more positive. He obviously didn't get that my main aim was just to cut down the number of syllables.

My mum tried her best to sound supportive (well, as much as you can when all your hopes and dreams for your first born are shattered in an instant). She hugged me and reminded me that I was 'good with kids'; I had done my work experience in a nursery after all. My name was added to the prayer chain, again. I sat some exams at eight months pregnant, despite the psych department being extremely concerned that my fail would look bad for their department on the prospectus.

Giving birth

At 2am, two days before the due date, contractions started. I went downstairs to watch MTV because I knew the hospital didn't want me wasting their time with false alarms. At 8am I decided to go into hospital. My son was born at 8.23am. Giving birth is absolutely the single most amazing thing in the world. I could not believe that there was a real, live baby at the end of this – a bloody baby! I instantly fell head-over-heels madly in love the second I saw him. I didn't want him in the cot next to me, I didn't want to sleep, ever; I just wanted to hold him. He was perfect. And I wasn't fat any more.

I squeezed back into my size eight jeans and took my perfect baby to college with me to pick up my results (which included an in-your-face-A in psychology) and managed to sort out going back part-time. They had never had to deal with a student who was a mother before but my tutor kindly sorted it out.

After a year she also helped me apply (last minute) for uni. She said anyone could go to this one, so long as you could climb the stairs. It sounded ideal. I was surprised by how little class time uni required. I could still go to all the parent and toddler groups and not miss out on the mummy stuff at all. I would then study through the night while my son slept. At 18, I got married and a few days before our one-year anniversary. But not long after, while my husband was at the shop, I put my son in his buggy, picked up his shoes and walked out. The relationship was doomed from day one. I just wasn't ready to be a single teenage mum. It sounded like I'd failed. Anyway, the divorce came through just after my 20th birthday.

I turned up on the doorstep of my patient, long-suffering parents. Even after what I'd put them through, they were still pleased to see me. The study became the toy room and the garden filled with swings and sandpits. My son soaked up all the attention. We shared a bunk bed and, at weekends, when he was fast asleep, I'd creep out and pretend to be that cute, little, innocent thing again for a few hours, although the innocent bit tended to wear off after the first hour. I quickly made up for my lost youth, or something like that. Looking back, I'm glad I did while I still had the energy and before my body knew about hangovers. You can scowl at me all you like, but I hadn't been allowed out for four years and, suddenly, I found myself with live-in babysitters urging me to go out and have fun. Deal with it. Besides, I was always back by morning.

I graduated at 21, my son started school and I got myself a crappy part-time job that often involved putting things in alphabetical order or colouring in, much like at home, but eventually I managed to find a bank that took into account family credit and child benefit when they calculated how much mortgage I could get. I felt like a millionaire. I think this is what's now referred to as irresponsible lending. Lucky for them, I was probably the most responsible 22-year-old they had ever met – at least with money anyway! Estate agents, however, saw a dizzy, young girl on her own with a child playing house, and ignored me. I resorted to knocking on the doors of houses with for sale signs to ask for a peek, till I finally found my house. My son got his own bedroom. A loyal friend, looking for a cheap place to live while she did her teacher training, paid half the bills. We were set up. Meanwhile I met a guy who was the complete opposite to me. He stole my lodger's ham once, so she had to move out. I eventually let him move in. He's very good at making people laugh and fixing things. I've spent too much time over the past 11 years wondering whether this is enough, but I guess this is all we really need. He's good at the things that I'm not good at, like knowing where my keys are, and has proved invaluable in emergency situations. I should stop worrying about it. Or have more emergencies.

By 26 I'd completed a master's, got a proper job, moved to a bigger house and bought a baby grand piano for £200 off eBay for my son. If you hadn't seen me ten years earlier, I could have been mistaken for someone who knew what she was doing.

At 33, I'm now officially a mother of a 16-year-old. I still think he is the most perfect thing ever. But I know I'm lucky; I'm lucky that my parents forgave me for not following the path they expected and that they turned out to be the best grandparents ever. I'm lucky that the birth of my son was timed nicely for the middle of the summer holidays, and that my college tutor was actually my fairy godmother in disguise. Maybe she was quick to land the Gift from God line on me when I turned up in her classroom at 16 in floods of tears (and she tells me now that when pregnant students seek her out she always checks what the girl wants to do first) but, to her credit, she did look after me when I needed it and now looks out for my son at the college as he starts his A-levels there. (Pro-lifers take note: if you can't promise at least 16 years of personal support, I say you should put your placard down and re-think your approach.)

Even now that I'm all grown up, we still don't look like your average family. When you find out that I'm meant to be responsible for this stunning 16-year-old towering above me, despite not looking much older myself, you may take a second before you decide on your reaction. Or you might not. But every young mum has her own story. This is just mine.

Promoting Respect for Young Mothers: Prymface

As I approached 30, and my son 13, I found that I still hadn't shaken off the dreaded 'teen mum' label. I still got looks from people when I mentioned my son's age. 'Oh, you were that kind of girl', their faces would say. I also noticed that while I was busy desperately trying to disassociate myself from the young mum stereotype, the reality was that all the young mums I knew were actually bloody amazing. Rather than being ashamed, I felt like they should feel proud of who they were and what they were doing. And actually, even though it felt weird, I was kind of proud of myself, too.

I started blogging as Prymface as a way to share a different side of young parenthood, as an alternative to the one-dimensional horror story many in the media prefer to portray. Prym stands for Promoting Respect for Young Mothers (and is a play on Pramface), and is about showing an alternative face of teen parenthood which challenges the common stereotype. I wanted to talk honestly about relationships and parenting without judgement or feeling that I was having to prove I was 'different to other teen mums'.

I blog anonymously so I can do that. Not because being a young mum is something to be ashamed of, but because our stories are often complex, and we should be allowed to choose what we share and who we share them with. Young parents are not a drama for your entertainment. We are not a cautionary tale to tell to your daughters. We are not your ego boost so that, even when you really mess up, you can still say 'well I least I wasn't a teen mum like her'.

Young mums deserve the same level of respect and support as any other parent. We should feel OK saying 'I'm proud of how hard I've worked to get my s*** together' instead of keeping our heads down in case we upset someone older or louder or more important than us.

But the reality is that people will see what they want to see. And so we protect ourselves. We try to fit in and not draw attention to ourselves. But underneath, we know. We know young mums kick a**. While you were nursing hangovers, rinsing student overdrafts and sleeping through your lectures, we were already well on our way to doing the most important job there is. You shouldn't need to know a young mum's entire life story to show her some respect. You just need to know that everything you thought you knew about teenage mums was probably based on ignorance and a little bit of prejudice. My blog tries to challenge those assumptions, and encourage young mums to hold their heads up high, without having to explain to people why.

3 October 2012

⇨ The above information is reprinted with kind permission from *The Telegraph*. Please visit www.telegraph.co.uk for further information.

Let's teach teenage girls to expect more than a baby

Boys need to be taught to be more responsible instead of girls taking the shame and blame as a result of a teenage pregnancy.

Teenage pregnancy rates in Scotland are, according to stats, among the highest in Europe.

In short, too many of our kids are having kids while hardly out of their gym slips – and sometimes while still in them. It's also a matter of class. You live in some posh suburb and you're four times less likely to have a baby than someone who comes from a deprived estate. But why?

Sex education is taught in all our schools and contraception is readily and freely available, so it can't just be sheer ignorance, can it?

There are those who argue that if, instead of teaching pupils about the mechanics, we concentrated more on abstinence, then the figures would fall.

Except we know from the States that doesn't work and indeed increases the chances not only of pregnancy but of a sexually transmitted infection.

We also know that those countries such as Holland, which are nothing like as half-hearted, embarrassed and hesitant about discussing sexual health with their kids, both in the home and their schools, don't have anything like our problem.

Nor is it simply a matter of getting the girls on the Pill or even sewing teenage boys into condoms the minute they hit puberty. Mind you, we do too often leave the lads out of the equation, as if these misconceptions had nothing whatsoever to do with them.

I wouldn't want to return to the days of sticking a shotgun up their rear ends, far less bring back the guilt and shame which, back in the dark ages, was wished on a woman who became pregnant without either a husband or wedding ring. But boys need to be taught to be more responsible.

There are still an awful lot of 'wee nyaffs' who, as one charmingly put it on TV the other night, don't bother too much about putting their 'wellies on'.

There are also girls who are so desperate for affection and lacking in self-esteem that they confuse sex with true love. What they think is a relationship is little more than a two-minute stand.

However, I've slowly become convinced that, for some, having a baby is almost a career choice. They look around them and there aren't too many other opportunities out there, so why not make motherhood a job?

And can you blame them when the right-wing media would have us – and more unforgivably the girls themselves – believe you have a baby and, abracadabra, you automatically get a nice new flat, limitless benefits and everything paid for.

Nor do the soaps – with their glammed-up vision of lone parenthood – help, where family and the wider community are invariably seen rallying round.

The reality for young single mums, as the majority find out way too late, isn't anything as cushy.

Being a single mum is hard at any age but in your teens it is a bed of thorns rather than roses. There's seldom enough money or proper support. It's lonely.

Sure, some will make brilliant mums but for others it's a dead end, a one-way street that leads to few opportunities and responsibility for another vulnerable life when their own has hardly begun.

Somehow, we've got to give them something else to aspire to.

11 January 2013

⇨ The above information is reprinted with kind permission from the *Daily Record* and *Sunday Mail*. Please visit www.dailyrecord. co.uk for further information.

Bringing education to young mothers through mobiles

The challenges of educational access for young Kenyan mothers present opportunities for mobile learning support.

By Ronda Zelezny-Green

As we celebrate the International Day of the Girl today, we should take time to remember that young mothers are still girls, too. We need to do what we can to support them in their educational endeavours – even in means considered to be non-traditional. Mobile learning might be one way we can support young mothers when school interruptions occur due to early pregnancy. Here are some of my thoughts which draw upon the Kenyan context.

Schooling and early pregnancy in Kenya

With a high rate of early pregnancies among women in Kenya, female children in both primary and secondary school are increasingly being affected. One of the most damaging side effects of this phenomenon in Kenya is that once pregnant, many girls face barriers such as a lack of awareness among school administrators about laws on early pregnancy and schooling, severe time constraints due to care work and even familial beliefs that deny them the right to continue their education.

Recently, speaking on education reform, cabinet secretary for education, science and technology in Kenya Jacob Kaimenyi drew attention to the difficulties that girls face when they want to return to school after having a baby. Although there is no policy in place that restricts a girl's ability to rejoin her peers in school, many girls drop out or are sent home when the pregnancy is discovered, are turned away when they try to return to school after giving birth or are refused the chance to try and return because of the stigma the pregnancy and subsequent birth places on the girl and her family.

Commonly there is a desire by girl learners to continue their education, especially their formal education, despite their pregnancy even when the barriers to returning to school imposed by their families or schools and social stigmas may not easily permit it. Awareness-raising campaigns about the rights of young mothers, such as the girl declaration, can undoubtedly help address issues surrounding access to education by young mothers. Nevertheless, problems persist, and for girls out of reach or otherwise unable to benefit from these mechanisms, mobile phones could offer learning support.

Despite the use of mobiles in a number of facets of Kenyan society (banking, utilities, retail, health, transportation, etc.), their use in education remains limited to a few offerings such as Eneza Education (mostly secondary) and eLimu (mostly primary).

Some of the oft-repeated challenges to mobile learning as a viable vehicle for education include the costs associated with ownership and maintenance of the devices, fears of inappropriate use and the alleged difficulty of reading on the devices with small screens.

While a study from Kenya indicated that some may go without food to own and maintain a mobile device, the device is often used to improve its owner's life, making the costs spent on its usage long-term investments. Eneza Education and gMaarifa demonstrate that high-end mobile devices and smartphones are not a necessary prerequisite for mobile learning in Kenya, since both organisations' approaches to mobile learning do not require more expensive mobile tools.

Inappropriate use of mobile devices is a common issue around the world among youth. Perceived and real problems can range from contacting a member of the opposite sex to cyberbullying. Yet, a knee-jerk reaction to this challenge is to ban youth mobile use altogether. Educating Kenyan girls – and their families – on potential pitfalls and guiding them to use mobile devices appropriately is more sensible, especially when they are likely to find a way to use the devices anyway. But we do not see many mobile learning initiatives globally making this an integral part of their approach, to the detriment of any possible long-term success.

Helping to dispel the notion that reading on mobiles is difficult, Worldreader adds evidence that reading in Kenya, even on small feature phones and eReaders, can be enjoyable and beneficial to young learners.

Education is key for marginalised girls (such as young mothers) to participate in all domains of the societies they live in. If an overarching goal for Kenya is to cultivate a knowledge economy, then more avenues of obtaining this knowledge need to be opened up for young mothers, a group that can contribute substantially to development efforts if given access to education.

Young mothers of school age in Kenya make ideal beneficiaries of mobile learning opportunities when they experience school interruptions because they have a strong need for flexibility when juggling the demands of child rearing, are not always able to attend school even if they are permitted to return, do not always have consistent or affordable access to formal education or computers, may feel embarrassed to return to school after giving birth, and can make use of the mobile literacy skills they gain to pursue income-generating activities, if needed.

What subjects can young mothers access through mobile-based instruction?

When girls leave school after becoming pregnant or are unable to return after giving birth, the stigma of exclusion compounds their marginalisation. But we are seeing encouraging signs of possible future support in bridging the home-school divide at the primary and secondary level with educational technology. Through mobile devices, we have seen a number of subjects taught including maths (Dr Math, M4Girls), mother tongue languages (eTaleem, MoToLi), science (Text2Teach), sexual health & HIV/Aids prevention (education as a vaccine) and life skills (learning about living).

For young mothers in Kenya, having support to access education at a distance, in the subjects above, which will be critical to their success as they grow into adults, should be viewed as a right and not a luxury. Mobile learning can be one medium to help realise this right. Nevertheless, even when this approach is undertaken, practitioners and educators must ensure they work to involve the girls' communities in the transformation process. Plan International has a number of resources for how community involvement in support of girls can be mobilised, including identifying community members who can be girl child champions. After all, it takes a village to raise a child.

Ronda Zelezny-Green is a member of the ICT4D collective at Royal Holloway, University of London. She tweets as @GLaM_Leo

11 October 2013

⇨ The above information is reprinted with kind permission from *The Guardian*. Please visit www.guardian.co.uk for further information.

Key facts

- In 1961, 38 per cent of families consisted of a married couple with two or more children. (page 1)

- Recent Scottish Widows data shows that today just 16 per cent of the UK population fit the 'traditional model'. (page 2)

- Nearly 89% of people think that an unmarried couple with children counts as a family, and 87% of people think that a lone parent with at least one child counts as a family. (page 2)

- 47% of people think that a same-sex couple in a civil partnership are a family. (page 2)

- In Asia and the Middle East, children under 18 are more likely to live in two-parent families, whereas children in the Americas, Europe, Oceania and Sub-Saharan Africa are more likely to live with one or no parent. (page 3)

- In Canada, 78 per cent of children live in two-parent households. (page 3)

- In South Africa, 43 per cent of children live in single-parent families. (page 3)

- Between 47 (Singapore) and 77 per cent (India) of the young adult population in Asian countries are married. (page 5)

- The average number of children born per woman in the UK is 1.9. In Bolivia, the average is 3.3. (page 5)

- In the year 2000, there were 600,000 live births in England. By 2010 this had risen to 723,165. (page 10)

- Mothers have got older. The average age of a mother in 1971 was 26.6, and this had risen to 29.3 in 2008. (page 10)

- The number of babies being born outside of marriage has increased sixfold over the past 40 years. (page 10)

- Lone parent families are increasing at a rate of 20,000 a year. (page 11)

- Each year, adoptive families are needed for some 4,000 children. (page 17)

- 26 per cent of step-parents that have their own biological children say that they can't help but compare the behaviour of their own children to that of their partner's. (page 22)

- Average family debt has peaked at almost £13,000, even though the average family income has increased by more than £1,200 a year. (page 25)

- 39% of British people say that they do not often have money for luxuries, but can normally cover the essentials. 4% cannot afford their costs and often have to go without essentials like food and heating. (page 27)

- 33% of new parents say that money worries are their main cause of stress. (page 28)

- The Relationships Foundation, a think-tank on relationships and society, calculated the cost of family breakdown as £46 billion in March 2013. (page 28)

- 32,000 women choose to stay at home to take care of their families. (page 29)

- Parents pay an average of £111 per month on school extras. (page 29)

- Only a third of single parents on benefit are actually receiving any child maintenance. (page 30)

- In 2010 the under-18 conception rate was 35.5 conceptions per 1,000 women. (page 32)

- In 2010, there was a 6.8% decline in conception rates among girls under 16 from 2009. (page 32)

Adoption

When a child is adopted, an individual or couple apply to become the child's parents. Once the court order is granted, the adopters become the child's legal guardians in the way that their birth parents previously were, and the biological parents cease to have any legal rights over the child.

This is different from fostering, where families will provide a stable home for children on a temporary basis. Although some children do stay with their foster family long-term, fosterers do not become the child's legal parents.

Cohabiting couple

Two people who live together as a couple but are not married or in a civil partnership. Current trends suggest more couples are choosing to have children in cohabiting rather than married relationships.

Child maintenance

Usually paid by the parent who is not the primary caregiver/day-to-day carer of the child. Designed to provide financial help toward's a child's everyday living costs. This can be organised through the Child Maintenance Service, but can also be agreed privately.

Child poverty

In order to live above the poverty line, a family with two adults and two children in the UK needs £349 each week to cover food, transport, shoes, clothes, activities, electricity, gas, water, telephone bills, etc.

Dependent children

Usually defined as persons aged under 16, or 16 to 18 and in full-time education, who are part of a family unit and living in the household.

Family

A domestic group related by blood, marriage or other familial ties living together in a household. A 'traditional' or nuclear family usually refers to one in which a married heterosexual couple raise their biological children together; however, changing family structures has resulted in so-called 'non-traditional' family groups including step-families, families with adopted or foster children, single-parent families and children being raised by same-sex parents.

Lone/single parent

Someone who is raising a child alone, either due to divorce/separation, widowhood, an absent parent or due to single adoption. The majority of lone parents are women.

Parental responsibility

When an adult has the legal right to take responsibility for the care and well-being of their child(ren) and can make important decisions about things such as food, clothing and education, this is referred to as parental responsibility. Married couples having children together automatically have this right, as do all mothers, but if the parents are unmarried the father only has parental responsibility if certain conditions are met.

Step-family

Step-families come together when people marry again or live with a new partner. This may be after the death of one parent, separation or divorce. It can also mean that children from different families end up living together for all or part of the time. One in four children has parents who get divorced and over half of their mothers and fathers will remarry or repartner to form a step-family.

Assignments

Brainstorming

⇨ In small groups, think of as many different family structures as you can, e.g. Mum, Dad and one or more children; Mum, Step-Dad and one or more children, etc. Draw pictures to demonstrate the different types of family you have named and create a poster to showcase your brainstorming session.

Research

⇨ In the UK today, the average number of children born per woman is 1.9. Has this number changed throughout history? Carry out some research and see what you can find out about the average number of children per family in different time periods throughout UK history. Draw a timeline to represent your research and feedback to your class.

⇨ Research the support available for teenage parents in your local area. Make a list of any support groups, charities or organisations that you discover and feedback to your class. Consider whether you think there is enough support available, and whether it is easily accessible.

⇨ Draw-up a budget for a family of two parents and two children. The children are aged six and 12. Write down everything you can think of that the family will need to pay for: living expenses, socialising, clothes, travel, accommodation, etc. How much money will the family need per week? How much is that per year? Discuss with your class.

Design

⇨ Design a leaflet for teenage dads, detailing where they can go for help and what they should expect when they become a father.

⇨ Design a poster that illustrates the different types of modern families identified in the article on pages 8 and 9.

⇨ Imagine that you are starting a charity that aims to promote the importance of grandparents' in a child's life – highlighting the help and support they often give. In small groups, think of a name for your charity and design a logo. If you want to take this further you could also design a homepage for your charity's website and write an introductory message about the aims of your organisation. Try reading the articles on pages 18 and 19 for support.

Oral

⇨ Think about your feelings towards marriage and divorce. Do you think you will get married in the future? Why do you feel you would or would not want this for yourself? What kind of wedding ceremony would you have if you were to get married? Discuss with a partner.

⇨ Read the article on pages 8 and 9 and, in small groups, discuss the different types of families that are identified. Do you think the article covers enough different types? Can you add some more to the list? Make some notes and feedback to the rest of your class.

⇨ Choose one of the illustrations from this book and, with a partner, discuss what you think the artist was trying to portray with the image.

⇨ As a class, stage a debate in which half of you argue that the term 'blended family' is a positive way of referring to families that contain step-parents or step-siblings and half of you argue that it is detrimental. If you are arguing that it is detrimental, you should think of some alternative terms that could be used.

Reading/writing

⇨ Why do you think so many fairytales feature 'evil' step-parents and siblings? Write your own modern fairytale, featuring a positive example of a step-family.

⇨ Think of some children's fiction you have read which portrays family situations, such as *Little Women* by Louisa May Alcott, the Famous Five books by Enid Blyton, the Harry Potter books by JK Rowling, the Tracy Beaker books by Jacqueline Wilson or *Wolf* by Gillian Cross. Choose at least two books which portray different types of families and write a comparative essay.

⇨ Watch the film *Stepmom*, starring Julia Roberts and Susan Sarandon then write a report discussing how the film represents various issues surrounding step-families.

⇨ Write a blog post exploring the importance of educating young mothers. Choose whether you would like to focus on young mothers in the UK or young mothers in Africa.

Index

Acknowledgements

The publisher is grateful for permission to reproduce the material in this book. While every care has been taken to trace and acknowledge copyright, the publisher tenders its apology for any accidental infringement or where copyright has proved untraceable. The publisher would be pleased to come to a suitable arrangement in any such case with the rightful owner.

Images

Cover and iii: iStock, page 6: iStock, page 10: iStock, page 14: iStock, page 18: iStock, page 22: iStock, page 24: iStock, page 30: iStock, page 32: anonymous, Flickr, page 37: istock, page 38 © Jacob Botter, page 39 © Piotr Lewandowski.

Illustrations

Pages 1 and 2: Simon Kneebone, pages 8 and 9: Don Hatcher, pages 16 and 20: Angelo Madrid.

Additional acknowledgements

Editorial on behalf of Independence Educational Publishers by Cara Acred.

With thanks to the Independence team: Mary Chapman, Sandra Dennis, Christina Hughes, Jackie Staines and Jan Sunderland.

Cara Acred

Cambridge, January 2014